Katharine Bundell is a senior barrister in private practice at 4PB. She specialises in financial remedy, and private law children including abduction with a long-standing background in trusts of land work. Much of her practice has an international flavour, a trusts element an/or complex corporate structures. She is a qualified Arbitrator (MCI Arb), a frequent mentor and a regular pupil supervisor. She often writes published articles, lectures for most of the main CPD providers and last year presented to the New York State Bar Association on the treatment of crypto currency in this jurisdiction.

A Practical Guide to Financial Provision for Children under Schedule 1 of the Children Act 1989

Second Edition

A Practical Guide to Financial Provision for Children under Schedule 1 of the Children Act 1989

Second Edition

Katharine Bundell, MA (Cantab) MCI Arb
Barrister-at-Law, 4PB
Advocacy, advice and lecturing
Financial Remedy and Private Law children

Law Brief Publishing

Published 2025 by Law Brief Publishing, an imprint of Law Brief Publishing Ltd
30 The Parks
Minehead
Somerset
TA24 8BT

www.lawbriefpublishing.com

Paperback: 978-1-916698-77-2

To my husband and children and all the family practitioners who have given time, support and advice to their colleagues over the years.

PREFACE

The current twist on the classic lawyer joke is Satan saying to the next customer: "I hope you're not a politician or a lawyer, because we need to diversify down here". This tired stereotype, which predates Shakespeare, is contrary to my personal experience. I have found our profession to be both supportive and kind to those who are under its aegis. There have been exceptions, especially in Court, when we all have our battle armour tied on tight, but many times in my career I have been assisted and supported by others whom I have approached for help. One senior barrister loaned me the money for my first car, another helped me feed twin babies in chambers, my first pupil would drive me everywhere in exchange for frequent food (he is 14 inches taller than me) and many others took time out of their days to answer my questions as I tapped gingerly on their doors, or sidled up to them in corridors. As I grew more experienced, I was able to provide some direction to those who came to ask me what they should do, or where they should look for an answer. Maybe we all like to answer questions but not everyone likes to ask.

This book is intended as a helpful commentary for those who do not undertake Schedule 1 cases on a regular basis and need to ask for some advice, or just want someone by their side who has done this before. It is not intended to be a definitive, learned and academic text. It is a practitioner's guide. You will need some experience of financial remedy work to understand the technical bits. It contains a number of helpful hints, lots of checklists, some of my practice points and strategies, and takes the law from first base. It sets out arguments you can run and challenges you can mount and where to find the authority to support your point. I take you into the basics of trusts of land cases which can so often both complement and counteract a Schedule 1 claim, but which also tend to give rise to anxiety in family practitioners who are not regular civil litigators.

The point of the book is to answer all of your basic questions, give you the technical tools and to help you to run a case with flair and confidence. It is also to encourage you to use the Schedule more often. Your local Judges will not stop feeling self-conscious in making awards unless you put more of these cases in front of them.

The law is taken as up to date at the 1st January 2025. The book was first written in the middle of the Brexit maelstrom and just before the pandemic. This is the right time for the second edition. There are things to report from the last few years, ranging from badly behaved oligarchs, through helpful judgments from Peel J and even a dalliance with conduct.

Katharine Bundell
January 2025

CONTENTS

CHAPTER ONE

INTRODUCTION: THE PURPOSE OF THIS GUIDE

Introduction: the purpose of this guide

Let us start, like a standard form ancillary relief order, with some definitions. This guide concerns claims for financial support for (usually) unmarried parents. I will call this type of claim "Schedule 1", as that appears to be its most common moniker amongst us. That comes from Schedule 1 of the Children Act 1989. The schedule is entitled "Financial Provision for Children". It contains almost all of the statutory material that you need.

This is intended to be a practitioner's guide. I have worked on the assumption that you have the level of knowledge of a family lawyer. By that, I mean that most if not all of your workload will be in the family law jurisdiction and some of that will include financial claims. You may be working at the independent Bar or in a firm, as a legal executive, trainee, newly qualified, newly requalified, restarter, care worn long timer or somewhere in between or to the side. Let us call ourselves "practitioners".

I am, I hope, one of you. I used to drag various graded sizes of trolley bag or rucksack to various courts or out of court resolution rooms most days of the working week, but our chambers has been paperless since before the pandemic. Now I take an extra tablet on which I have downloaded my bundles. I do this in the context of a family with 3 children, and a supportive spouse and dog, who have grown around the singular demands of what we do.

You cannot have worked long as a practitioner in this jurisdiction without having provided some free advice or assistance to a colleague or co-practitioner. I have found ours the most supportive and collaborative jurisdiction. I have often been the recipient of such advice, both personal and professional, from those older, younger, more experienced or just more insightful, and I have usually been improved by it. I hope I have been able to respond in kind to the email which starts like a gentle tap on the door with "KB, can I just run something past you?". We often work more remotely now. This is beneficial for those with caring or other responsibilities, and it reduces travel, which can be burdensome and expensive, but we are not so often in the office or chambers, able to bounce ideas around while standing by the kettle. This guide is intended to assist in answering some of those queries, both general and specific, that might occur when running one of these cases. I have focussed upon the practical questions about the filing in of forms, the focus of the arguments and the presentation and interrogation of evidence. Schedule 1 cases are not the most common cases we run in the family courts and many of us go years without seeing one. Most practitioners therefore feel the need to ask a question, if only to confirm our understanding or hunch.

If you are an experienced family law specialist practitioner or academic, then this book may not be useful to you. I have presumed a certain level of practical knowledge, but I do not profess to have written this guide as an academic paper or a guide for big money cases. This is a guide for the majority of cases which travel through the family courts. Financial support for children of unmarried parents has been concerning courts, the church, the poor law and parishes for a long time. It is not a new phenomenon. The cases for which this guide may assist could involve large sums, but not original points of law or complex corporate structures.

The Children Act 1989 was a reforming piece of legislation introduced in the Queen's Speech of November 1988, during a Thatcher government. It codified a patchwork of other statutes and brought public and private law under one statute. It did away with the notion of parental rights and replaced it with the concept of parental responsibilities. It introduced the welfare checklist at s 1(3) of the Children Act 1989. The children at the centre of the statute were to have their wishes and feelings considered as a free-standing factor. This reflected the changes in society over the previous 3 decades. It was ahead of its time in many ways. Like the Matrimonial Causes Act 1973, it is a tribute to those who work in our jurisdiction that they were able to draft legislation that is sufficiently flexible and sensitive to be able to stay the course of time and seismic changes in social attitudes. Often, statutes appear at the back of a book or not at all. I am putting this statute at the front of the guide to encourage you to always refer back to it. The schedule is introduced by section 15 in the Act. Schedule 1 is comprehensive. Whatever your question about its scope, it is likely that the answer is in there.

I have also included a level of supporting case law so that you can understand why I state the law as I do and explain to those with a different view (who may sometimes be the Judge) why your point is made. You may wish to quote it to make a slightly different point, or you may interpret it differently, but I hope it assists in the structuring of your argument. Case law is important in this area as there is only one significant piece of statutory material and so previous examples of the interpretation of that statute and application of the discretion it confers, can assist. There are not so many cases in the law reports concerning Schedule 1, so you have to be aware of context inflation and changing social attitudes. One of the features of the application of precedent is that no two factual situations are ever exactly the same and so caution has to be exercised, particularly in this area, not to take as an absolute the outcome of one case and impose it onto another without considering context. The application of the discretion can explain how different factors interact and the weight they may carry, or new ideas for how a situation has been resolved. They will rarely give you a complete answer to the order which a Court would make, because of a factual parallel. The seminal cases will give you a sense of how and why the statutory discretion is applied and others will illustrate how to resolve sone of the modest asset cases or more unusual situations and some more straightforward cases give you chance to use your new knowledge to guess before the end what the outcome might be.

Having these cases or arguments in your armoury should be as useful for the hostile cases as much as for finding areas of agreement, or more attractive bi-partisan solutions in cases which have some potential for settlement. Explaining and supporting your point is relevant for both. This may be especially so in Schedule 1 cases which often pull into their orbit trusts of land disputes about beneficial interests in property: the parties are often previously cohabiting unmarried parents so I have touched upon the basics of these at the end of the book, because they so often arise and are so unpalatable to so many. Running a case which encompasses a trusts of land claim in the civil jurisdiction and a Schedule 1 claim in the family jurisdiction may be complex within the currently over-stretched court system and so these cases lend themselves particularly well to non-court dispute resolution. I have also therefore included a section on non-court dispute resolution ("NCDR") for Schedule 1 (and beyond) which is usually the more constructive approach for clients who have to continue to parent together and who cannot divorce themselves from that attachment.

The "Schedule 1" case is often called the Cinderella in our jurisdiction. That is Cinderella before the ballgowns and glass slippers. I don't know that I agree save to the extent that Schedule 1 has indeed been one of the least loved sections of the behemoth that is the Children Act 1989. Many practitioners, and some judges, seem to avoid it, concerned by its procedure or limitations or feel it is only of use in large money cases. I am here to encourage you to take your Schedule 1 knowledge out of the back of the wardrobe more often, and to feel you can use it more readily if the issues fit. Whether for families of modest means, or cases with previously married parents, child maintenance service cases or high incomes: Schedule 1 should not just be for special occasions.

CHAPTER TWO

THE STATUTE

SECTION 15(1) CHILDREN ACT 1989

Orders for financial relief with respect to children.

(1) Schedule 1 (which consists primarily of the re-enactment, with consequential amendments and minor modifications, of provisions of section 6 of Family Law Reform Act 1969 the Guardianship of Minors Acts 1971 and 1973, the Children Act 1975 and of sections 15 and 16 of the Family Law Reform Act 1987) makes provision in relation to financial relief for children.

SCHEDULE 1 CHILDREN ACT 1989

Financial Provision for Children

(1) Orders for financial relief against parents

1. (1) On an application made by a parent, guardian or special guardian of a child, or by any person who is named in a child arrangements order as a person with whom a child is to live, the court may make one or more of the orders mentioned in sub-paragraph (2).

(a)..............................

(b)..............................

(2) The orders referred to in sub-paragraph (1) are—

(a) an order requiring either or both parents of a child—

(i) to make to the applicant for the benefit of the child; or

(ii) to make to the child himself,

such periodical payments, for such term, as may be specified in the order;

(b) an order requiring either or both parents of a child—

(i) to secure to the applicant for the benefit of the child; or

(ii) to secure to the child himself,

such periodical payments, for such term, as may be so specified;

(c) an order requiring either or both parents of a child—

(i) to pay to the applicant for the benefit of the child; or

(ii) to pay to the child himself,

such lump sum as may be so specified;

(d) an order requiring a settlement to be made for the benefit of the child, and to the satisfaction of the court, of property—

(i) to which either parent is entitled (either in possession or in reversion); and

(ii) which is specified in the order;

(e) an order requiring either or both parents of a child—

(i) to transfer to the applicant, for the benefit of the child; or

(ii) to transfer to the child himself,

such property to which the parent is, or the parents are, entitled (either in possession or in reversion) as may be specified in the order.

(3) The powers conferred by this paragraph may be exercised at any time.

(4) An order under sub-paragraph (2)(a) or (b) may be varied or discharged by a subsequent order made on the application of any person by or to whom payments were required to be made under the previous order.

(5) Where a court makes an order under this paragraph—

(a) it may at any time make a further such order under sub-paragraph (2)(a), (b) or (c) with respect to the child concerned if he has not reached the age of eighteen;

(b) it may not make more than one order under sub-paragraph (2)(d) or (e) against the same person in respect of the same child.

(6) On making, varying or discharging... a special guardianship order, or on making, varying or discharging provision in a child arrangements order with respect to the living arrangements of a child, the court may exercise any of its powers under this Schedule even though no application has been made to it under this Schedule.

(6A) For the purposes of sub-paragraph (6) provision in a child arrangements order is with respect to the living arrangements of a child if it regulates arrangements relating to—

(a) with whom the child is to live, or

(b) when the child is to live with any person.

7) Where a child is a ward of court, the court may exercise any of its powers under this Schedule even though no application has been made to it.

(2) Orders for financial relief for persons over eighteen

2(1) If, on an application by a person who has reached the age of eighteen, it appears to the court—

(a) that the applicant is, will be or (if an order were made under this paragraph) would be receiving instruction at an educational establishment or undergoing training for a trade, profession or vocation, whether or not while in gainful employment; or

(b) that there are special circumstances which justify the making of an order under this paragraph,

the court may make one or both of the orders mentioned in sub-paragraph (2).

(2) The orders are—

(a) an order requiring either or both of the applicant's parents to pay to the applicant such periodical payments, for such term, as may be specified in the order;

(b) an order requiring either or both of the applicant's parents to pay to the applicant such lump sum as may be so specified.

(3) An application may not be made under this paragraph by any person if, immediately before he reached the age of sixteen, a periodical payments order was in force with respect to him.

(4) No order shall be made under this paragraph at a time when the parents of the applicant are living with each other in the same household.

(5) An order under sub-paragraph (2)(a) may be varied or discharged by a subsequent order made on the application of any person by or to whom payments were required to be made under the previous order.

(6) In sub-paragraph (3) "periodical payments order" means an order made under—

(a) this Schedule;

(b) . . . .

(c) section 23 or 27 of the Matrimonial Causes Act 1973;

(d) Part I of the Domestic Proceedings and Magistrates' Courts Act 1978,

(e) Part 1 or 9 of Schedule 5 to the Civil Partnership Act 2004 (financial relief in the High Court or a county court etc.);

(f) Schedule 6 to the 2004 Act (financial relief in the magistrates' courts etc.),

for the making or securing of periodical payments.

(7) The powers conferred by this paragraph shall be exercisable at any time.

(8) Where the court makes an order under this paragraph it may from time to time while that order remains in force make a further such order.

(3) Duration of orders for financial relief

3(1) The term to be specified in an order for periodical payments made under paragraph 1(2)(a) or (b) in favour of a child may begin with the date of the making of an application for the order in question or any later date or a date ascertained in accordance with sub-paragraph (5) or (6) but—

(a) shall not in the first instance extend beyond the child's seventeenth birthday unless the court thinks it right in the circumstances of the case to specify a later date; and

(b) shall not in any event extend beyond the child's eighteenth birthday.

(2) Paragraph (b) of sub-paragraph (1) shall not apply in the case of a child if it appears to the court that—

(a) the child is, or will be or (if an order were made without complying with that paragraph) would be receiving instruction at an educational establishment or undergoing training for a trade, profession or vocation, whether or not while in gainful employment; or

(b) there are special circumstances which justify the making of an order without complying with that paragraph.

(3) An order for periodical payments made under paragraph 1(2)(a) or 2(2)(a) shall, notwithstanding anything in the order, cease to have effect on the death of the person liable to make payments under the order.

(4) Where an order is made under paragraph 1(2)(a) or (b) requiring periodical payments to be made or secured to the parent of a child, the order shall cease to have effect if—

(a) any parent making or securing the payments; and

(b) any parent to whom the payments are made or secured,

live together for a period of more than six months.

(5) Where—

(a) a maintenance calculation ("the current calculation") is in force with respect to a child; and

(b) an application is made for an order under paragraph 1(2)(a) or (b) of this Schedule for periodical payments in favour of that child—

(i) in accordance with section 8 of the Child Support Act 1991; and

(ii) before the end of the period of 6 months beginning with the making of the current calculation,

the term to be specified in any such order made on that application may be expressed to begin on, or at any time after, the earliest permitted date.

(6) For the purposes of subsection (5) above, "the earliest permitted date" is whichever is the later of—

(a) the date 6 months before the application is made; or

(b) the date on which the current calculation took effect or, where successive maintenance calculations have been continuously in force with respect to a child, on which the first of those calculations took effect.

(7) Where—

(a) a maintenance calculation ceases to have effect or is cancelled by or under any provision of the Child Support Act 1991, and

(b) an application is made, before the end of the period of 6 months beginning with the relevant date, for an order for periodical payments under paragraph 1(2)(a) or (b) in favour of a child with respect to whom that maintenance calculation was in force immediately before it ceased to have effect or was cancelled,

the term to be specified in any such order, or in any interim order under paragraph 9, made on that application may begin with the date on which that maintenance calculation ceased to have effect or, as the case may be, the date with effect from which it was cancelled, or any later date.

(8) In sub-paragraph (7)(b)—

(a) where the maintenance calculation ceased to have effect, the relevant date is the date on which it so ceased; and

(b) where the maintenance assessment was cancelled, the relevant date is the later of—

(i) the date on which the person who cancelled it did so, and

(ii) the date from which the cancellation first had effect.

(4) Matters to which court is to have regard in making orders for financial relief

4(1) In deciding whether to exercise its powers under paragraph 1 or 2, and if so in what manner, the court shall have regard to all the circumstances including—

(a) the income, earning capacity, property and other financial resources which each person mentioned in sub-paragraph (4) has or is likely to have in the foreseeable future;

(b) the financial needs, obligations and responsibilities which each person mentioned in sub-paragraph (4) has or is likely to have in the foreseeable future;

(c) the financial needs of the child;

(d) the income, earning capacity (if any), property and other financial resources of the child;

(e) any physical or mental disability of the child;

(f) the manner in which the child was being, or was expected to be, educated or trained.

(2) In deciding whether to exercise its powers under paragraph 1 against a person who is not the mother or father of the child, and if so in what manner, the court shall in addition have regard to—

(a) whether that person had assumed responsibility for the maintenance of the child and, if so, the extent to which and basis on which he assumed that responsibility and the length of the period during which he met that responsibility;

(b) whether he did so knowing that the child was not his child;

(c) the liability of any other person to maintain the child.

(3) Where the court makes an order under paragraph 1 against a person who is not the father of the child, it shall record in the order that the order is made on the basis that the person against whom the order is made is not the child's father.

(4) The persons mentioned in sub-paragraph (1) are—

(a) in relation to a decision whether to exercise its powers under paragraph 1, any parent of the child;

(b) in relation to a decision whether to exercise its powers under paragraph 2, the mother and father of the child;

(c) the applicant for the order;

(d) any other person in whose favour the court proposes to make the order.

(5) In the case of a child who has a parent by virtue of section 42 or 43 of the Human Fertilisation and Embryology Act 2008, any reference in sub-paragraph (2), (3) or (4) to the child's father is a reference to the woman who is a parent of the child by virtue of that section.

(5) Provisions relating to lump sums

5(1) Without prejudice to the generality of paragraph 1, an order under that paragraph for the payment of a lump sum may be made for the purpose of enabling any liabilities or expenses—

(a) incurred in connection with the birth of the child or in maintaining the child; and

(b) reasonably incurred before the making of the order,

to be met.

(2) . . . .

(3) The power of the court under paragraph 1 or 2 to vary or discharge an order for the making or securing of periodical payments by a parent shall include power to make an order under that provision for the payment of a lump sum by that parent.

(4) . . . .

(5) An order made under paragraph 1 or 2 for the payment of a lump sum may provide for the payment of that sum by instalments.

(6) Where the court provides for the payment of a lump sum by instalments the court, on an application made either by the person liable to pay or the person entitled to receive that sum, shall have power to vary that order by varying—

(a) the number of instalments payable;

(b) the amount of any instalment payable;

(c) the date on which any instalment becomes payable.

(7) The Lord Chief Justice may nominate a judicial office holder (as defined in section 109(4) of the Constitutional Reform Act 2005) to exercise his functions under this paragraph.

(6) Variation etc. of orders for periodical payments

6(1) In exercising its powers under paragraph 1 or 2 to vary or discharge an order for the making or securing of periodical payments the court shall have regard to all the circumstances of the case, including any change in any of the matters to which the court was required to have regard when making the order.

(2) The power of the court under paragraph 1 or 2 to vary an order for the making or securing of periodical payments shall include power to suspend any provision of the order temporarily and to revive any provision so suspended.

(3) Where on an application under paragraph 1 or 2 for the variation or discharge of an order for the making or securing of periodical payments the court varies the payments required to be made under that order, the court may provide that the payments as so varied shall be made from such date as the court may

specify, except that, subject to sub-paragraph (9), the date shall not be earlier than the date of the making of the application.

(4) An application for the variation of an order made under paragraph 1 for the making or securing of periodical payments to or for the benefit of a child may, if the child has reached the age of sixteen, be made by the child himself.

(5) Where an order for the making or securing of periodical payments made under paragraph 1 ceases to have effect on the date on which the child reaches the age of sixteen, or at any time after that date but before or on the date on which he reaches the age of eighteen, the child may apply to the court which made the order for an order for its revival.

(6) If on such an application it appears to the court that—

(a) the child is, will be or (if an order were made under this sub-paragraph) would be receiving instruction at an educational establishment or undergoing training for a trade, profession or vocation, whether or not while in gainful employment; or

(b) there are special circumstances which justify the making of an order under this paragraph,

the court shall have power by order to revive the order from such date as the court may specify, not being earlier than the date of the making of the application.

(7) Any order which is revived by an order under sub-paragraph (5) may be varied or discharged under that provision, on the application of any person by whom or to whom payments are required to be made under the revived order.

(8) An order for the making or securing of periodical payments made under paragraph 1 may be varied or discharged, after the death of either parent, on the application of a guardian or special guardian of the child concerned.

(9) Where—

(a) an order under paragraph 1(2)(a) or (b) for the making or securing of periodical payments in favour of more than one child ("the order") is in force;

(b) the order requires payments specified in it to be made to or for the benefit of more than one child without apportioning those payments between them;

(c) a maintenance calculation ("the calculation") is made with respect to one or more, but not all, of the children with respect to whom those payments are to be made; and

(d) an application is made, before the end of the period of 6 months beginning with the date on which the calculation was made, for the variation or discharge of the order,

the court may, in exercise of its powers under paragraph 1 to vary or discharge the order, direct that the variation or discharge shall take effect from the date on which the calculation took effect or any later date.

(6A) Variation of orders for periodical payments etc. made by magistrates' courts

6A (1) Subject to sub-paragraph (7), the power of the family court—

(a) under paragraph 1 or 2 to vary an order for the making of periodical payments, or

(b) under paragraph 5(6) to vary an order for the payment of a lump sum by instalments,

shall include power, if the court is satisfied that payment has not been made in accordance with the order, to exercise one of its powers under section 1(4) and (4A) of the Maintenance Enforcement Act 1991.

(2) . . . .

(3) . . . .

(4) . . . .

(5) . . . .

(6) Subsection (6) of section 1 of the Maintenance Enforcement Act 1991 (power of court to order that account be opened) shall apply for the purposes of sub-paragraph (1) as it applies for the purposes of that section.

(7) Before varying the order by exercising one of its powers under section 1(4) and (4A) of the Maintenance Enforcement Act 1991, the court shall have regard to any representations made by the parties to the application.

(8) . . . .

(9) None of the powers of the court ... , conferred by this paragraph shall be exercisable in relation to an order under this Schedule for the making of periodical payments, or for the payment of a lump sum by instalments, unless at the time when the order was made the person required to make the payments was ordinarily resident in England and Wales.

(10) . . . .

(7) Variation of orders for secured periodical payments after death of parent

7(1) Where the parent liable to make payments under a secured periodical payments order has died, the persons who may apply for the variation or discharge of the order shall include the personal representatives of the deceased parent.

(2) No application for the variation of the order shall, except with the permission of the court, be made after the end of the period of six months from the date on which representation in regard to the estate of that parent is first taken out.

(3) The personal representatives of a deceased person against whom a secured periodical payments order was made shall not be liable for having distributed any part of the estate of the deceased after the end of the period of six months referred to in sub-paragraph (2) on the ground that they ought to have taken into account the possibility that the court might permit an application for variation to be made after that period by the person entitled to payments under the order.

(4) Sub-paragraph (3) shall not prejudice any power to recover any part of the estate so distributed arising by virtue of the variation of an order in accordance with this paragraph.

(5) Where an application to vary a secured periodical payments order is made after the death of the parent liable to make payments under the order, the circumstances to which the court is required to have regard under paragraph 6(1) shall include the changed circumstances resulting from the death of the parent.

(6) The following are to be left out of account when considering for the purposes of sub-paragraph (2) when representation was first taken out—

(a) a grant limited to settled land or to trust property,

(b) any other grant that does not permit any of the estate to be distributed,

(c) a grant limited to real estate or to personal estate, unless a grant limited to the remainder of the estate has previously been made or is made at the same time,

(d) a grant, or its equivalent, made outside the United Kingdom (but see sub-paragraph (6A)).

(6A) A grant sealed under section 2 of the Colonial Probates Act 1892 counts as a grant made in the United Kingdom for the purposes of sub-paragraph (6), but is to be taken as dated on the date of sealing.

(7) In this paragraph "secured periodical payments order" means an order for secured periodical payments under paragraph 1(2)(b).

(8) Financial relief under other enactments

8(1) This paragraph applies where a child arrangements order to which sub-paragraph (1A) applies or a special guardianship order is made with respect to a child at a time when there is in force an order ("the financial relief order") made under any enactment other than this Act and requiring a person to contribute to the child's maintenance.

(1A) This sub-paragraph applies to a child arrangements order if the arrangements regulated by the order consist of, or include, arrangements which relate to either or both of the following—

(a) with whom the child concerned is to live, and

(b) when the child is to live with any person.

(2) Where this paragraph applies, the court may, on the application of—

(a) any person required by the financial relief order to contribute to the child's maintenance; or

(b) any person who is named in a child arrangements order as a person with whom the child is to live or in whose favour ... a special guardianship order with respect to the child is in force,

make an order revoking the financial relief order, or varying it by altering the amount of any sum payable under that order or by substituting the applicant for the person to whom any such sum is otherwise payable under that order.

(9) Interim orders

9(1) Where an application is made under paragraph 1 or 2 the court may, at any time before it disposes of the application, make an interim order—

(a) requiring either or both parents to make such periodical payments, at such times and for such term as the court thinks fit; and

(b) giving any direction which the court thinks fit.

(2) An interim order made under this paragraph may provide for payments to be made from such date as the court may specify except that, subject to paragraph 3(5) and (6), the date shall not be earlier than the date of the making of the application under paragraph 1 or 2.

(3) An interim order made under this paragraph shall cease to have effect when the application is disposed of or, if earlier, on the date specified for the purposes of this paragraph in the interim order.

(4) An interim order in which a date has been specified for the purposes of sub-paragraph (3) may be varied by substituting a later date.

(10) Alteration of maintenance agreements

10(1) In this paragraph and in paragraph 11 "maintenance agreement" means any agreement in writing made with respect to a child, whether before or after the commencement of this paragraph, which—

(a) is or was made between the father and mother of the child; and

(b) contains provision with respect to the making or securing of payments, or the disposition or use of any property, for the maintenance or education of the child,

and any such provisions are in this paragraph, and paragraph 11, referred to as "financial arrangements".

(2) Subject to sub-paragraph (2A), where a maintenance agreement is for the time being subsisting and each of the parties to the agreement is for the time being either domiciled or resident in England and Wales, then, either party may apply to the court for an order under this paragraph.

(2A) If an application or part of an application relates to a matter in relation to which Article 18 of the 2007 Hague Convention applies, the court may not entertain the application or that part of it except where permitted by Article 18.

(2B) In sub-paragraph (2A), "the 2007 Hague Convention" means the Convention on the International Recovery of Child Support and Other Forms of Family Maintenance concluded on 23 November 2007 at The Hague.

(3) If the court to which the application is made is satisfied either—

(a) that, by reason of a change in the circumstances in the light of which any financial arrangements contained in the agreement were made (including a change foreseen by the parties when making the agreement), the agreement should be altered so as to make different financial arrangements; or

(b) that the agreement does not contain proper financial arrangements with respect to the child,

then that court may by order make such alterations in the agreement by varying or revoking any financial arrangements contained in it as may appear to it to be just having regard to all the circumstances.

(4) If the maintenance agreement is altered by an order under this paragraph, the agreement shall have effect thereafter as if the alteration had been made by agreement between the parties and for valuable consideration.

(5) Where a court decides to make an order under this paragraph altering the maintenance agreement—

(a) by inserting provision for the making or securing by one of the parties to the agreement of periodical payments for the maintenance of the child; or

(b) by increasing the rate of periodical payments required to be made or secured by one of the parties for the maintenance of the child,

then, in deciding the term for which under the agreement as altered by the order the payments or (as the case may be) the additional payments attributable to the increase are to be made or secured for the benefit of the child, the court shall apply the provisions of subparagraphs (1) and (2) of paragraph 3 as if the order were an order under paragraph 1(2)(a) or (b).

(6) . . . .

(7) For the avoidance of doubt it is hereby declared that nothing in this paragraph affects any power of a court before which any proceedings between the parties to a maintenance agreement are brought under any other enactment to make an order containing financial arrangements or any right of either party to apply for such an order in such proceedings.

(8) In the case of a child who has a parent by virtue of section 42 or 43 of the Human Fertilisation and Embryology Act 2008, the reference in sub-paragraph (1)(a) to the child's father is a reference to the woman who is a parent of the child by virtue of that section.

(11)

11(1) Where a maintenance agreement provides for the continuation, after the death of one of the parties, of payments for the maintenance of a child and that party dies domiciled in England and Wales, the surviving party or the personal representatives of the deceased party may apply to the High Court or the family court for an order under paragraph 10.

(2) If a maintenance agreement is altered by a court on an application under this paragraph, the agreement shall have effect thereafter as if the alteration had been made, immediately before the death, by agreement between the parties and for valuable consideration.

(3) An application under this paragraph shall not, except with leave of the High Court or the family court, be made after the end of the period of six months beginning with the day on which

representation in regard to the estate of the deceased is first taken out.

(4) The following are to be left out of account when considering for the purposes of sub-paragraph (3) when representation was first taken out—

(a) a grant limited to settled land or to trust property,

(b) any other grant that does not permit any of the estate to be distributed,

(c) a grant limited to real estate or to personal estate, unless a grant limited to the remainder of the estate has previously been made or is made at the same time,

(d) a grant, or its equivalent, made outside the United Kingdom (but see sub-paragraph (4A)).

(4A) A grant sealed under section 2 of the Colonial Probates Act 1892 counts as a grant made in the United Kingdom for the purposes of sub-paragraph (4), but is to be taken as dated on the date of sealing.

(5) . . . .

(6) The provisions of this paragraph shall not render the personal representatives of the deceased liable for having distributed any part of the estate of the deceased after the expiry of the period of six months referred to in sub-paragraph (3) on the ground that they ought to have taken into account the possibility that a court might grant leave for an application by virtue of this paragraph to be made by the surviving party after that period.

(7) Sub-paragraph (6) shall not prejudice any power to recover any part of the estate so distributed arising by virtue of the making of an order in pursuance of this paragraph.

(12) Enforcement of orders for maintenance

12(1) Any person for the time being under an obligation to make payments in pursuance of any order for the payment of money made by the family court under this Act shall give notice of any change of address to such person (if any) as may be specified in the order.

(2) Any person failing without reasonable excuse to give such a notice shall be guilty of an offence and liable on summary conviction to a fine not exceeding level 2 on the standard scale.

(3) . . . .

(13) Direction for settlement of instrument by conveyancing counsel

13 Where the High Court or the family court decides to make an order under this Act for the securing of periodical payments or for the transfer or settlement of property, it may direct that the matter be referred to one of the conveyancing counsel of the court to settle a proper instrument to be executed by all necessary parties.

(14) Jurisdiction

14 (1) The court has jurisdiction in relation to an application under paragraph 1 in respect of a child if any of the following persons are habitually resident or domiciled in England and Wales on the date of the application—

(a) parent of the child;

(b) a guardian or special guardian of the child;

(c) a person who is named in a child arrangements order as a person with whom the child is to live;

(d) the child.

(2) The court has jurisdiction in relation to an application under paragraph 2 if the applicant or a parent against whom the order is sought or made is habitually resident or domiciled in England and Wales on the date of the application.

(15) Local authority contribution to child's maintenance

15(1) Where a child lives, or is to live, with a person as the result of a child arrangements order, a local authority may make contributions to that person towards the cost of the accommodation and maintenance of the child.

(2) Sub-paragraph (1) does not apply where the person with whom the child lives, or is to live, is a parent of the child or the husband or wife or civil partner of a parent of the child.

(16) Interpretation

16(1) In this Schedule "child" includes, in any case where an application is made under paragraph 2 or 6 in relation to a person who has reached the age of eighteen, that person.

(2) In this Schedule, except paragraphs 2 and 15, "parent" includes—

(a) any party to a marriage (whether or not subsisting) in relation to whom the child concerned is a child of the family, and

(b) any civil partner in a civil partnership (whether or not subsisting) in relation to whom the child concerned is a child of the family;

and for this purpose any reference to either parent or both parents shall be read as a reference to any parent of his and to all of his parents.

(3) In this Schedule, “maintenance calculation" has the same meaning as it has in the Child Support Act 1991 by virtue of section 54 of that Act as read with any regulations in force under that section.

CHAPTER THREE

SCHEDULE 1 AND STATUTORY CHILD SUPPORT: A DOUBLE ACT?

This legislation is underused. I seek to explain here its origins and objectives. It was the warmup act for the Child Support Act 1991, but it can be so much more than the big-name headline went on to achieve. The two statutes have a shared history and connection. Schedule 1 can assist in many cases where the CMS has not been enough.

In 1989, only 20 years after a revolution in divorce law, the Children Act 1989 was passed by Parliament. It introduced not just the enlightened concepts of residence and contact, parental responsibility and the voice of the child but codified financial support for unmarried parents before the Child Support Act 1991 introduced state collection of child maintenance.

If you had looked back at recent history when Schedule 1 was being drafted, what would you have seen? The Children Act 1989 was passed only 20 years after the Divorce Reform Act 1969 which introduced the concept of divorce based upon "*irretrievable breakdown of marriage*". Consideration of this similarly ground-breaking legislation paints a clear picture of the trajectory of family law at the time. Before the Divorce Reform Act 1969 came into effect in 1971, divorce could only be granted to a woman on the basis that she had proved, through her sworn evidence, adultery, drunkenness, incurable insanity or desertion on the part of her husband. The husband had more options at his disposal, but divorce was still a matter of contentious litigation demanding evidence and proof. Readers of John Mortimer may remember the stories he told of his blind barrister father on the train, listening intently to his wife read out loud the contents of various salacious divorce statements: the responding party would book a hotel, and the petitioner would send an enquiry agent to report upon the presumed adultery as "Mr and Mrs Smith" booked in for the night. The agent would duly report back to the petitioner, who could then present the confected evidence in support of the petition to end the unhappy marriage. The parties often had to work in concert if they were to achieve a divorce. This unfairness needed to be addressed. After the Second World War, society had begun to change quickly. Marriages struggled under the weight of emotional baggage following war time experiences and periods of separation and independence. There had been a Royal Commission on the issue of reform in the 1950s but it had struggled to make recommendations. In the 1960s, the Archbishop of Canterbury took up the challenge and convened a group which came to support the concept of no-fault divorce. After long years of discussion and debate about the effect upon us as a society, finally the law was changed. The 1969 Act was a major piece of social legislation, eventually passed by the second Wilson government. It took persistence, hard politics and careful planning. For the first time it allowed parties to divorce by consent after 2 years of separation, or without consent, on the application of one party alone, after 5 years of separation. For the first time divorce was possible without proving fault.

Then came the 1970s, a time of further dramatic social change and huge economic instability. It was not until 1987 that the Bastardy Acts were repealed, which had codified the different treatment and recognition of children born in and out of wedlock. It had taken 69 years of campaigning to secure this step towards equality for the children of different unions.

The commencement of the Children Act 1989 is now more than 30 years ago. It was conceived and honed in a time which for me holds memories of the rah-rah skirt and electric blue eyeliner, a Saturday treat 7" vinyl single and hair-sprayed new romantic pop bands whose posters were stuck on my wardrobe door. The alternative comedy scene was highly political, and most people were engaged in or by politics. Our families were different, as well as our dress sense. Our Grandparents had lived through the Second World War and our parents had grown up in a time when the teenager and young adult was struggling to assert themselves as a singular but recognisable stage of life. Children of the eighties still heard epithets such as “children should be seen and not heard” and “spare the rod and spoil the child”. Corporal punishment was used enthusiastically in most schools. Few families yet broke out of the gender stereotypes and children’s books confirmed the bias. LGBTQI+ acceptance was in the minority and gay parents were viewed with suspicion and a widespread lack of understanding. However, social change was starting to shout about itself. The dungarees, bovver boots and short hair marked out the gay pride campaigners who were determined to support the largely conservative Welsh miners during the pit closures and many of the Top of the Pops appearances challenged the understanding of the generations above us as to the parameters of sexuality and gender. In the cities, brick-sized mobile telephones were being brandished by Yuppies, excitedly celebrating the Stock Exchange’s Big Bang and share ownership for everyone as the utility companies floated. Sloane Rangers in velvet Alice bands and designer clothes appeared in magazines and acquisition became an aspiration. North Sea oil money continued to flow.

At the other end of the economic spectrum, welfare spending was escalating and the Thatcher government was keen to pursue a managed “housekeeping” budget. In 1989 it was said that 70% of lone parents were in receipt of Income Support and the cost of meeting the bill for welfare benefits had tripled during the nineteen eighties. There was a caricature in certain parts of the press of the benefit dependant, lone parent who was more take than give. The demographic may have been changing but lone parenthood, a burden usually carried by mothers, was still treated with stigma rather than support in many parts of society. There was far less childcare provision, far fewer nurseries and no free childcare vouchers. Child minders were not regulated. There was no working and child tax credit yet, only child benefit and part time working was often not financially viable or available around school holidays.

The thinking behind state collected child support

There are figures which suggest that at the time of these new Acts, only 30% of lone parents and 22% of lone parents claiming benefit were in receipt of child support from a non-resident parent. The government was committed to shrinking the state, so needed to think of ways to reduce the perceived benefit dependency and simplify the means of collection of child support. Child support was ordered by the Courts, so there was little consistency, limited accessibility to the system, and it was enforced by the Department of Social Security. Legal Aid was of course still available for parents to issue court proceedings but that involved further government funding. Often the sums involved were mediocre compared to the cost of securing them and the cost/benefit analysis showed that this was not economically viable in the longer term. The intention of those legislating was to empower resident parents to take action themselves, to reduce child poverty and, with the support of the state for enforcement, for the non-resident parent to do the right thing and pay, so relieving the taxpayer of that burden.

A different system

As an example of a different approach, albeit in a country with a far smaller population, I learned from one case I advised upon that in Norway the government will step in and pay child support if a non-resident parent does not. In that case the non-resident parent was a British citizen living in England and the child and resident parent were Norwegian, living in Norway. When the child attained 18 years of age the Norwegian state totted up the entire child maintenance bill it had paid to the resident parent over the years, added some interest and registered it for enforcement in the English magistrates' court local to the parent who had not paid. The non-resident parent (who had never met the child) got a surprising summons for an even more surprising amount to their local Court.

The start of the Child Support Act 1991 legislation

Back in the UK in 1990 the government issued a white paper called *Children Come First* which proposed a system of centralised child support collection based upon a statutory formula and the removal of the Court process, save in very limited cases. This gave rise to the Child Support Act of 1991 which in turn gave birth to the Child Support Agency which opened its doors and turned on its computers in 1993. It attracted much criticism from an early stage. Its remit was to calculate what a non-resident parent ought to pay, to collect that money and then to transfer it to the resident parent. There were strict rules set out in the Child Support Act 1991 about the circumstances in which the child support agency could and could not make an assessment.

Child support formulae and the 3 systems

The Child Support Agency had 2 sets of formulae and criteria it applied, cases from 1993 and later and cases from 2003 and later, and then the Child Maintenance Service applied a 3rd set of criteria and a different formula again for cases from 2012.The Independent Case Examiner's Office was set up in 1997 as an independent body to deal with complaints about the Child Support Agency. The main complaints were delay, error and lack of action but it also had serious problems with poor communication, bad management and poor outcomes for payer and payee. The complaints came from both the payer and the payee. Despite the Child Support Agency opening in 1993, the 1990s saw little change in that figure of only 30% of unmarried lone parents receiving any financial support from the non-resident parent. A Joseph Rowntree study in 1996 looked at 53 low-income lone parent families. Not one had been assisted by the legislation and a quarter of those families had suffered a negative impact upon its relationship due to problems caused by using the service.

In 1997 the New Labour government began to reform the system and the Child Support, Pensions and Social Security Act 2000 was passed.

These new reforms went live in March 2003 along with a new method of assessment. By 2006 a government policy evaluation found that of 670,000 cases where the non-resident parent had been assessed as having a liability, only 400,000 could show money being paid which then reached the resident parent. There was a backlog of 300,000 cases and £3bn of uncollected debt. Still only 30% of lone single parents received any child maintenance from the non-resident parent and only 15% of those in receipt of Income Support received any maintenance through the Child Support Agency. There was little evidence of changes in the numbers of receiving parents from when the Courts had been seised of the matter back in the 1980s. Eventually the Child Support Agency, and its enforcement arm the Child Maintenance and Enforcement Commission were replaced in 2012 by the Child Maintenance Service and its enforcement arm the Child Maintenance Group, under the coalition government. This led to yet another set of collection rules, this time based upon the payer's gross salary as evidenced by the documents held by HMRC. Service users were encouraged to move old cases onto the new rules. This took 6 years and the last cases were moved over in late 2018.

The current formula

This is the system now available to users. The basic formula is applied to the payer's gross income after pension payments and is 12% for one child, 16% for 2 children and 19% for 3 or more children. There are deductions for having children in the payer's household or paying child support for other children, and the nights the children in question stay with the payer. If there is exactly equal and shared care then there is no child support payable (equal care is a decision of fact, definition cf Regulation 50 Child Support Maintenance Calculation Regulations 2012 and cases such as DW v Secretary of State for Work and Pensions (CMS) and JH [2023] UKUT 19 (AAC)).

There is a child maintenance calculator on the government website.

How the current system is working

There is a useful House of Commons paper dated 18th December 2024 titled Child Maintenance Service statistics. In 2022–2023 in England, Scotland and Wales around 59% of separated parents were found to have a child maintenance arrangement.

The default option is the *direct pay service*, where parents arrange payment between themselves. The Department for Work and Pensions conducted a survey of direct pay users between 2017–19. It found three months after a direct pay calculation, 85% of parents with care said they either had or were setting up a child maintenance arrangement. There is also *collect and pay* where the CMS collects payments themselves and passes them on. Both parents pay for this. In the quarter to September 2024 only 68% of parents under collect and pay made any form of payment at all, although 85% of those were compliant.

The service can use *collection actions* which are powers it already has or *enforcement* powers which come from a liability order which the service secures from the Court. In the quarter to September 2024 the English and Welsh Courts imposed 140 prison sentences, 1 passport confiscation order, and 2 driving licence disqualification orders for non payment of child support including arrears.

The Children Act 1989 Schedule 1 can help in many cases. It is not designed to be used only in unusual circumstances. It is legislation that was born out of the intention to assist all separated parents in a changing society and it has certainly not been rendered otiose by the child support legislation which was drafted to reduce the state's welfare bill but which has been singularly unsuccessful in its early years and still struggles to meet the needs of many today.

CHAPTER FOUR

HOW DOES SCHEDULE 1 DIFFER FROM FINANCIAL REMEDY?

Financial remedy cases start with a consideration of entitlement to sharing of marital acquest or capital and then adjustment from sharing, if required, to meet needs and/or fairness. Schedule 1 of the Children Act 1989 empowers the court to award financial provision to or for the benefit of a child but based upon the child's needs only, not the adult's needs, unless they overlap (although some cases of large awards may stretch that concept to the outer limits of its elasticity). There is no entitlement to sharing of assets or income under Schedule 1.

This is all perhaps best described by the following judgment extract discussing the remit of Schedule 1:

Example Authority

PG v TW (No 2) (Child: Financial Provision) [2014]1 FLR 923 per HHJ Horowitz QC:

> *"25. The Court's discretion in deciding whether and how to exercise its powers is guided by a six-point checklist which has parallels with but is narrower than s25 of the Matrimonial Causes Act 1973. Regard must be had to all the circumstances of the case including, present or foreseeably likely finances, needs, obligations and responsibilities of the parent and child, the financial needs of the child and the manner in which the child is being or expected to be educated and trained.*

> *26. Thus there is no express reference to the contribution the parties have made or are likely to make or to the standard of living enjoyed prior to the breakdown of the marriage/relationship or its duration."*

The second main difference in the two schemes is that after divorce the parent or sometimes an adult child may apply for support if "extension conditions" are met. Under Schedule 1 the system is more complex with a form of baton passing when the child attains 18 years, so that provision for an adult child who satisfies the extension conditions because they are still in education or training or special circumstances apply, is only available on an application by the child themselves.

As noted by HHJ Hess[1] whilst the schemes do have differences these do not necessarily amount to discrimination against the children of unmarried parents and the scheme should be interpreted with the intention of there being no discrimination: "*...the remedies (as between the children of married and unmarried parents) can be different without necessarily amounting to unlawful discrimination, but that it is appropriate for any ambiguities to be construed purposively with the overall scheme of non-discrimination in mind.."*

In the same vein, the circumstances of a child's birth are irrelevant to a Schedule 1 order[2].

Ordinarily the Schedule 1 powers are invoked by unmarried parents, but marriage does not exclude the jurisdiction (see next chapter).

There is no 'no order principle', such as for child arrangement applications at section 1(5) of the Children Act 1989 where an order is only made if necessary.

---

1 *J & K v L (Schedule 1: Older Children)* [2021] EWFC B104 para 20 agreeing with Williams J in *DN v UD* [2020] EWHC 627, successfully appealed on other grounds in *UD v DN* [2021] EWCA Civ 1947

2 J v C (Child: Financial Provision) [1999] 1 FLR 152

The "welfare" of the child is not a paramount consideration under Schedule 1 nor is it the court's first consideration as with s 25 Matrimonial Causes Act 1973. Welfare is instead "*a constant influence*"[3].

Like with financial remedy, if the CMS has made an assessment, then the jurisdiction of the Court to make a Periodical Payments Order (maintenance) is largely by-passed. If the CMS has made an assessment that the payer earns more than the maximum cap (£3K per week after pension contributions)[4], the court can make a "top up maintenance order", in addition to child support. There is clear case law about continuing to apply the same CMS formula to the gross income, in excess of the maximum. If the CMS has made an assessment, or is seised of the case, and the assessment of the payer's income is below the maximum £3,000 per week cap, then the only Court order available, which is not really maintenance, is one for school fees.

Only where the CMS has no jurisdiction and has not been asked to deal with the case, can the court make a straightforward periodical payments order. As Moor J set out succinctly in *Tony Stacey v Lucy McNicholas [2022] EWHC 278* at paragraphs 27 and 35:

"Section 8(1) of the Child Support Act 1991 applies in any case where a child support officer has jurisdiction to make a maintenance assessment. Section 8(3) states that, in any case where subsection (1) applies, no court shall exercise any power which it would otherwise have to make, vary or revive any maintenance order in relation to the child and absent parent concerned. There are, of course, exceptions, such as where a maximum assessment has been obtained; the child is undertaking education and the order is made solely for the purpose of meeting some or all of the expenses incurred; the child is disabled; or one party resides overseas....

3 RE P [2003] EWCA Civ 837

4 *Dickson v Rennie 2014 EWHC 4306 (Fam)*

35. I entirely accept that the decision in Dixon v Rennie is correct. The court cannot "top-up" a CMS assessment unless there is a maximum assessment"

Watch out for the tricksy cases where a payer is living abroad but pays themselves through an English registered company such that they bring themselves within the CMS jurisdiction.

The Schedule 1 checklist

Section 25 of the Matrimonial Causes Act 1973 applies criteria for financial provision upon divorce. Under Schedule 1 of the Children Act 1989, paragraph 4(1) sets out the checklist which must be considered when assessing a claim:

'The Court must have regard to *"all the circumstances of the case"* including:

> *(a) the income, earning capacity, property and other financial resources which each person mentioned in sub-paragraph (4) has or is likely to have in the foreseeable future;*
>
> *(b) the financial needs, obligations and responsibilities which each person mentioned in sub-paragraph (4) has or is likely to have in the foreseeable future;*
>
> *(c) the financial needs of the child;*
>
> *(d) the income, earning capacity (if any), property and other financial resources of the child;*
>
> *(e) any physical or mental disability of the child;*
>
> *(f) the manner in which the child was being, or was expected to be, educated or trained."*

Practical Differences in Awards

The difference in the exercise of the discretions in practice is most obviously illustrated by the very few judgments for outright transfers of property under Schedule 1: property settlement is almost always ordered, rather than property transfer. Settlement is where the property is provided for the use of the resident parent and child(ren) but it reverts to the payer after the child has finished, say, tertiary education and their gap year. Property transfer is transferring a property to a resident parent outright and forever.

Payment of lump sums is commonly ordered to pay down debts which are hampering a parent from being able to afford to live, to buy a car or refurbish a property, but not to purchase a property save in very few cases, usually of exceptional wealth.

Differences in Preparation

There is therefore no need to fret about dates of cohabitation or who brought what into the relationship, nor any concept of marital acquest. If it is clearly agreed that there are sufficient assets to meet the child's needs, then it might not be necessary to nail down every last asset value, share option or pension detail. It is difficult to remember that sometimes when a Form E1 arrives full of holes, but the case only needs to take shape around provision for the child's reasonable needs.

However, aside from the difference in approach, the actual format of the process should feel very familiar to financial remedy practitioners. It is also governed by Part 9 of the Family Proceedings Rules 2010, so the forms are the same, as are the format of hearings.

CHAPTER FIVE

THE SCOPE OF THE CLAIM

You will usually find the answers to your questions about the scope of Schedule 1 within the legislation. However, before you commence any application or once you receive a request or claim on behalf of a respondent, you need to make sure that the applicant's aspirations fit within the criteria of what the court can award. This is quite detailed legislation and there is a level of complexity in the sections, and their interaction. However, if the legislation is still proving a little opaque you might not be alone: there have been a number of wide-ranging judgments on the scope of the legislation in recent months and we will look at those later.

There is jurisdiction to use Schedule 1 after marriage, even if there are claims still available under the Matrimonial Causes Act 1973 (or Civil Partnership Act 2004) and even if there has been an income and/or capital clean break order although it will be factor in the court's exercise of is discretion[5].

In one recent case[6] the parties had been married a short time, had a child and divorced with a simple income and capital clean break order, prohibiting any further financial claims. The mother committed a criminal offence against the child who moved to live with Father. He then made a valid claim against the Mother under Schedule 1 for a lump sum. The circumstances in which the court will use Schedule 1 to make a further lump sum payment after a clean break financial remedy order

5 MB v KB[2007] EWHC 789

6 TK v LK [2024] EWFC 71 cf para 53 et seq

have to be *"exceptional"*, but were found to be so in this case and an order was made in favour of the Father as carer.

When a client presents, be that as potential or actual applicant or respondent, it is always worth as a first step undertaking four specific checks.

Initial Pre Proceedings Checklist

(i) the scope of the legislation: can the court order what the client wants to achieve, or what is sought in the application;

(ii) do the parties have what I was taught to call *locus standi:* who are the right parties and do they qualify to make the claim against the named or proposed respondent;

(iii) should any other parties (such as an older child applicant) be added as a party to the claim;

(iv) should any other claim be issued (see next chapter).

CHAPTER SIX

QUICK GUIDE TO WHAT ORDERS CAN BE MADE UNDER SCHEDULE 1

The range of possible financial provision orders comprises:

- periodical payments (maintenance);
- secured periodical payments;
- lump sums;
- settlements of property; and
- transfers of property.

There is a Schedule 1 order precedent at form 2.2 under the standard financial and enforcement order templates on the judiciary website and it is useful to read as an aide memoire.

Checklist of Useful and Unusual Applications under Schedule 1 and beyond

Schedule 1 applications have various features which differ from financial remedy cases. Here is a list of some of the less usual circumstances which you might need or encounter:

- don't forget you can apply for a **Legal Services Payment Order** in Schedule 1 cases, for the wealthier party to pay a lump sum or monthly payments to assist the financially weaker party to fund their (usually future) legal representation so there is equality of arms; the criteria remains almost the same as for financial remedy[7]; you do not use the Matrimonial Causes At 1973, but you do use the same case law;

- a **freezing order** can be sought if there is clear evidence of unjustified dealing or threats of dealing with assets by the respondent which gives rise to the conclusion there is a solid risk of dissipation which would prejudice their ability to meet the claim[8]; this is sought under s 37 of the Supreme Court Act 1981, rather than s 37 of the Matrimonial Causes Act 1973 , as in financial remedy;

- a court can make **repeat orders for lump sums and periodical payments** (para 1(5) Schedule 1), but only one order about property (settlement or transfer);

- **if there is a financial relief order in place made OTHER than under Schedule 1** (usually made upon divorce) and the court makes any lives with order for child arrangements concerning with whom a child is to live and when, or a special guardianship order, then the court can make an order for financial provision under Schedule 1 at the time it makes the child arrangements order; **it can vary the order or substitute payee/payer** (para 8);

- **if the court is making, varying or discharging a special guardianship order, or a lives with child arrangements order as to with whom the child is to live and when, or making any order about a child who is a ward of court,** then the court can make a

7 *Rubin v Rubin* [2014] EWHC 611 (Fam) cf paragraph 13 for the criteria and JK v LM [2024] EWHC 1442 (Fam) per Cobb J para 24 et seq for a more recent example of this order in a Schedule 1 case

8 Per Mostyn J in *UL v BK* [2013] EWHC 1735 (Fam) at para 51

Schedule 1 order of its own motion with no application; (para 1(6));

- Per HHJ Hess[9] *"it does not follow ..... that awards cannot properly be made (if justified on the merits) against* ***paying parents of more modest wealth,*** *even where all or most of the available capital is needed to provide a home for a child."*

- the court may make a **lump sum or property order payable to a resident parent for a child who is over 18 years** of age by the time of its order, or at the time of payment, provided that the *application* for the order had been made before they reached that age[10]; maybe a parent has lost their job, fallen into debt, the mortgage is now unaffordable, or a new car is needed or the child has plans, such as for a Masters and a student loan is not available or insufficient to over the fees;

- there can be **payment of periodical payments for a child over the age of 18 years,** or to extend beyond their 18th birthday, by the application of what HHJ Hess calls the "*extension conditions*"[11]: if the child is still in education or training (even if also in work) or are there special circumstances (para 3(2) Schedule 1);

- if an adult child who satisfies the "extension conditions" wishes to make an application for periodical payments or a lump sum, they cannot do so if there was a periodical payments orders in

---

9 *SP v QR* [2024] EWFC 57 (B) at para 13

10 *UD v DN (Schedule 1, Children Act 1989; Capital Provision)* [2021] EWCA Civ 1947 and later referenced in *J&K v L (Schedule 1: Older Children)* [2021] EWFC B104 paragraphs 26/27 per HHJ Hess.

11 *J&K v L (Schedule 1: Older Children)* [2021] EWFC B104 para 27 and cf para 3(2) of Schedule 1

place immediately before they attained 16 years of age (paras 2 (1)(2)(3));

- **a child aged 16 yrs** or more may **apply to vary** a periodical payments order already made in favour of the resident parent (para 6 (4));

- an **adult child may apply to vary** a lump sum or periodical payments order made under **paras 2(1)(2)** on an application made by them as an adult;

- **if a periodical payments order has expired on a date when the child is between 16–18 years, then the child themselves can apply to revive that periodical payments order;** if the order expires after the child's 18th birthday (cf the usual formula, upon the child attaining 18 years and leaving secondary education) this does not apply; this can be useful in ancillary relief cases, where an order has lapsed and the court has no power in those ancillary relief proceedings to consider reviving an order which has finished (para 6(5)(6));

- paragraph 7 of Schedule 1 deals with the situation upon the **death of either payer or payee where there is still an order in force.**

CHAPTER SEVEN

THE PARTIES

The Parties

You may wish to consider whether your potential applicant qualifies to make the application (*locus standi,* as we used to call it in the days of regular Latin). Do look at this carefully, as there are a number of potholes.

If the parties are cohabiting, then there is no claim. I know it sounds unusual, but I am eternally surprised at the different situations which clients find themselves in, especially during pandemic restrictions or with high interest and mortgage rates. I had a case recently where one party ran an argument that the parties did not cohabit until 18 months after marriage, and 6 months after the first child arrived as they were unable to sell their sole name properties in a very expensive area of the country, and so were living financially separate lives and just having sleepovers at each other's property.

Applicant

There is jurisdiction to make an order if one of the following is either habitually resident or domiciled in England and Wales at the time of the application (para 14):

- natural or step-parent (para 16 (2)) of the child in question;
- guardian of the child;
- special guardian of the child;

- person with whom the child "lives" under a child arrangements order (or a pre-April 2014 residence order) or otherwise;[12]

- the child.

(therefore application may be made for a child living outside of the jurisdiction if the paying parent is domiciled/ habitually resident here)

FURTHER:

- the child for whom support is sought by a parent/ carer should be under 18 years (s105(1)) at the time of the application;

- the child for whom a periodical payments order is sought must be living with the applicant, although an application for housing can be made by a non-resident parent[13];

- the applicant could be the child who is between the ages of 16 and 18 years, if there was a periodical payments order in force for their benefit before that child's 16th birthday and is this is an application to vary or revive that order;

- the applicant could be the child who has attained 18 yrs old ONLY IF[14]:

12 *N v C (Financial Provision; Schedule 1 Claims Dismissed) 2013 EWHC 399 (Fam)*

13 *N v C [2013] EWHC 399 considering Re S (Child Financial Provision) [2005] 2 FLR 94*

14 Para 2(1)

  - they are, will be or would be if an order made, receiving education at an establishment or undergoing training for a trade, profession or vocation; OR

  - there are special circumstances; AND

  - there was no periodical payments order in force before their 16th birthday;

  - the application is for a lump sum and/or periodical payments, not a property order.

FURTHER

- there is no jurisdiction if the parents are cohabiting with each other (para 2);

A periodical payments order can only be made in favour of a child (as set out above) or the adult with whom the child lives. In *Re C* a variation of an order was sought which had been previously made when the child was living with mother, and now was living with father.

Example Authorities

In *MT v T [2006] EWHC 2494* Charles J referred to the judgment of Thorpe LJ in *Re S (Unmarried Parents: Financial Provisions) [2006] EWCA Civ 479*, and commented that it was difficult to square the welfare-based jurisdiction of the courts under Schedule 1 with the paucity of cases in which the voice of the child is heard, and reminded practitioners to give consideration to separate representation of the child.

Her Royal Highness Haya Bint Al Hussein V His Highness Mohammed Bin Rashid Al Maktoum [2021] EWFC 94

High profile series of judgments for enormous award to mother and children living in London made against Father who was ruler of Dubai and lived in the Middle East, and whilst instructing lawyers here refused to give evidence or attend any hearing.

N v C (Financial provision: Schedule 1 Claims Dismissed) [2013] EWHC 399 (Fam)

The child was aged 12 years and had lived with her mother. When P, the child, was young her father had applied to the court for parental responsibility and the parents had signed a manuscript agreement that the father had provided and would continue to provide a property for the mother and P. The parents had never married.

The mother issued her Schedule 1 proceedings, and the father applied for child arrangements. By the end of those proceedings the child had moved to live with her father. The mother continued with her Schedule 1 application for financial provision. The father was worth £3m and the mother had little capital in her name. She sought an order to confirm she was entitled to remain in the property in which she had always resided with P, and which he had promised her in the earlier agreement, but she conceded now P was not living with her that the property should be put in trust until P reached 18 years old or ceased full time education. In addition, she sought a lump sum of £200,000 to pay for renovations and substantial ongoing periodical payments of £2,200/month. She brought her claim on the basis either that P would return to live with her or that she must have a home to enjoy contact with P and the financial resources to run it. The Judge found as a fact that P was unlikely to return to her care.

The court found that there was no jurisdiction to make a maintenance order (Section 8 of the Child Support Act 1991 and the reality of P's child arrangements). The father's high income which might have triggered a top up order was immaterial given he had no liability to pay child support because the child was not living with her mother, but with him, her father.

The court found it had jurisdiction to make a financial order for capital under Schedule 1 against a resident parent in favour of a non-resident parent, by considering the case of *Re S (Child Financial Provision)* [2005] 2 FLR 94 but it noted that this has been rarely exercised and such an order would be unusual. The Court warned (the mother) and other parents against making claims pursuant to Schedule 1 which in effect were for the benefit of the parent, rather than the child.

Save for the exceptional circumstances such as the variation of the order made to a previously resident parent set out under variation of capital provision above, there should be no doubt that non-resident parents will not be entitled to bring a claim for maintenance and claims for capital will be exceptional.

Respondent

The respondent can be:

- either or both natural parents of the child, if the child is applying[15];
- the parent of a child who has been treated as a "child of the family" by them[16] but cf Blended Families below[17];
- the person who has liability to pay child support pursuant to the Child Support Act 1991;

---

15 Para 2(2)

16 Para 16(2)

17 Morgan v Hill

- the child may be a child who has been treated as a "child of the family"[18];

- the child MUST have a biological/adoptive connection[19] to the respondent OR have a connection through marriage/civil partnership and be a child of the family.

Paragraph 4 (2) (a–c) requires the court to consider:

> *"a) whether that person had assumed responsibility for the maintenance of the child, and, if so, the extent to which and basis on which he assumed that responsibility and the length of the period during which he met that responsibility;*
>
> *b) whether he did so knowing that the child was not his child;*
>
> *c) the liability of any other person to maintain the child."*

Checklist of Tips

- The court may make such an order of its own motion if it is making or varying or discharging a special guardianship order or any provision as to "living with" arrangements in a child arrangements order[20];

- The court may make an order at any time including of its own motion when the child is a ward of court[21];

---

18 S105(1) Children Act 1989

19 *T v B [2010] 2 FLR 1966*

20 Para 1(6)

21 Para 1 (7)

- a child can still bring proceedings e.g. for tertiary education fees[22] against either or both biological parents, adoptive parents, or parties who treated them as a child of the family; If the child is 16–18yrs the application is more simple; if the child is 18 years or over it is important to check there was no periodical payments order in effect for the benefit of this child before the child's 16th birthday and the extension conditions apply;

- If the parents are cohabiting together there is no claim;

- Any periodical payments order properly made shall cease to have effect if the payee and payer cohabit for more than 6 months;

- Under para 12 of Schedule 1 it is an offence for a payer not to give notice of change of address to the payee during the currency of an order.

---

22 *MB v KB 2007 2 FLR 586*

CHAPTER EIGHT

BLENDED FAMILIES AND MORGAN V HILL [2007]1FLR 1480

Nowadays blended families are a very common feature of our caseload. Often child arrangements and financial support work around more than one parent combination in a family. There may be grandparent carers, a new partner may arrive into a home with children of their own, who live some or all of the time with that parent or the applicant parent may have a dependent child with more than one partner. How is this relevant to Schedule 1? One of the most sensitive issues for a practitioner may be trying to gently tease apart what financial support is intended for or benefits which child. Of course, a Schedule 1 application is intended to be made against the non-resident parent of a biological/adopted child or child of the family and is to be for the benefit of that child only.

We need to consider the seminal case of *Morgan v Hill [2007]1FLR 1480, CA* in some detail as it deals with a number of important issues. It is so important, particularly to the modern day family, that it deserves its own chapter.

This case has three interesting strands of argument:

i. Variation of a previous maintenance agreement under Schedule 1: can this be considered as similar to an application under section 37 of the Matrimonial Causes Act 1973;

ii. Did the previous agreement made by the parents of the child, negotiated between solicitors, have a similar standing to a post nuptial agreement;

iii. Did the original order benefit the older child who was not the appellant's child, so the step sibling of the subject child? In this case the father, Stephen, appealed to the Court of Appeal against an order which he said benefitted Mary, who was not his child.

I will give you the background facts so you can understand the family set up.

First child

Janet was a highly educated and intelligent woman who was working in Paris in a leading financial institution when she had a relationship with a married man, Mr P, who was a fellow employee. She gave birth to their daughter Mary on 25th June 1997. They did not marry or cohabit, and he remained living out of our jurisdiction. Mary did not see her father and he sought no contact with her. In her turn, Janet did not seek any financial support from Mary's father for her at this time.

Second child

This position was possibly influenced by the fact that Janet Hill entered into a relationship with Stephen Morgan in 1998, so the year after Mary was born. Stephen was 14 years Janet's senior and described by Thorpe LJ as "*immensely rich*". During their time together Stephen financially supported Janet. He arranged for her to relocate back to the UK, working for a company in which he had a substantial interest. This did not last long, however, as when the relationship became public she was unable to continue to work there and she had been unemployed since 1998. Stephen had supported Janet and thereby Mary, who was not his child. He had helped Janet buy a cottage with her sister so she had somewhere to live in the UK. The property had been renovated by Janet's employer company and Stephen engineered a £30,000 discount in the price to Janet and her sister. The property was heavily mortgaged.

First Award for Mary

In 1999 Janet had begun proceedings pursuant to Schedule 1 in her local family (then county) court against Mr P, Mary's father and was awarded periodical payments of £4,160 pa or £80 per week.

First Agreement for Mark

The relationship with Stephen Morgan was not long lived and in 2000 it broke down. Janet was just pregnant with Mark who was born on 29th December 2000. By May 2000, so not long after Mark was conceived, informal talks had started about financial provision for the baby who would not appear for some months yet. However, these talks broke down within a few months. Heavyweight solicitors had been hired on both sides. Stephen made it clear that he would not pay for Mary, whatever had been the position during the relationship. The parties had not cohabited, so Mary had not been treated as a child of the family by Stephen. A complex but concluded agreement was reached in August 2001 providing for a trust document to be drawn up and it showed the parties had agreed as follows:

a) Stephen would buy out Janet's sister's share of her cottage which would be held on trust by Janet and Stephen in equal shares (Janet holding her interest subject to her mortgage);

b) if Janet moved within 5 years this was to be at her own cost; thereafter Stephen may contribute;

c) if Janet married or co-habited that would bring the trust to an end, unless Janet secured a Court order to say otherwise;

d) if Janet moved house, then the trust would not necessarily end, even if she were cohabiting, but she would pay rent for living in Stephen's part of the property;

e) Stephen was to pay Janet periodical payments at £39,000pa (index linked) until Mark attained 18 years and finished secondary education, being divided as to £16,000 for Mark and £23,000 for Janet's carer's allowance;

f) there was provision for reduction in periodical payments should Janet remarry, cohabit or return to work: if she cohabited then she lost the carer's element of her periodical payments and if she worked then she lost 50p in the pound of her allowance;

g) Stephen to pay Mark' school fees;

h) Stephen to provide an allowance for a car every 5 years and £100 pcm towards the running costs;

i) Stephen to make a contribution towards housing (at £115,000) including a mechanism by which Stephen would match any capital contribution by Janet towards a new property.

The agreement was expressed to be comprehensive and to make provision for the foreseeable future. Neither party pressed for the agreement to be converted into a court order although the concept was touched upon in correspondence.

Increased provision for Mary

In 2002 Janet applied against Mr P (Mary's father) for an increase in the periodical payments order. In 2003 the matter was compromised on the basis that periodical payments be increased to £12,000 pa and that Mr P cover Mary's school fees which to date had been paid by Stephen.

Increased provision for Mark

Three years after the agreement, Janet moved to a newly built house worth £382,500. To enable her to do so, she invested her share of the proceeds of sale of the cottage and took out a larger mortgage of £225,000. This resulted in her holding a 65% share in the property as opposed to Stephen's 35% share. However, the combination of moving costs and the burden of the bigger mortgage when she was not working, drove her into debt. She made an application for financial relief against Stephen under Schedule 1 of the Children Act 1989 on 17 January 2005. At trial her debts amounted to £96,503.

At first instance the Judge ordered a settlement of property worth £700,000 for Mark's minority *(which would not have been possible if the first agreement had been made into a court order, as there can only be one property order for each child).* He accepted Janet's case that the family needed a property in the country with paddocks and stables to enable them to pursue their passion for riding. Stephen was ordered to pay a lump sum of £100,000 to cover Janet's debts and his liability for periodical payments was increased from £39,000 to £60,000 pa. Therefore, together with £12,000 pa from Mary's father Janet received £72,000pa plus child benefit and school fees on top. The motor allowance was increased to £25,000 every 5 years.

On appeal, the Court noted from Janet's counsel, "*Mr Cayford has conceded that the judge's orders lie at the top end of the generous ambit of his discretion*". The appellant, Stephen, relied on two points of principle.

Firstly, that because the parties had negotiated the complicated and comprehensive agreement in 2001, before Mark had been born, and they had signed it with the assistance of their solicitors, this was a binding agreement, somewhat akin to a post nuptial agreement, and was a factor of magnetic importance. The agreement had been expressed in terms that the parties intended it to be final and comprehensive and a settlement of all her claims. Janet, he said, had failed to identify any factor which voided the agreement. The Court considered that section 10 of Schedule 1 mirrored section 37 of the Matrimonial Causes Act 1973 as to varying nuptial agreements.

Paragraph 10(3) reads as follows

> *"(3) If the court to which the application is made is satisfied either-*
>
> *a) That, by reason of a* ***change in the circumstances*** *in the light of which any financial arrangements contained in the agreement were made (including a change foreseen by the parties when making the agreement), the agreement should be altered so as to make different financial arrangements; or*
>
> *b) That the agreement* ***does not contain proper financial arrangements with respect to the child,***
>
> *Then that court may by order make such alterations in the agreement by varying or revoking any financial arrangements contained in it as may appear to it to be just having regard to all the circumstances."*

Thorpe LJ considered:

> *"Whether a claim is brought under paragraph 1 or 10 of the Schedule, the first hurdle is that the pre-existing agreement must be demonstrated to be either unenforceable given the circumstances surrounding its creation or, as the judge here found,* ***inadequate in its extent.****"*

Clearly the circumstances surrounding the creation of the agreement will largely reflect the principles of post nuptial agreements. However, Thorpe LJ provided that the test to be applied as to insufficiency could not depart from the statute, namely the inadequacy of the bargain in providing for the child's needs was still a good test. That was the case as the first instance Judge found it to be here. The Court was also clear that this case could have been brought as a freestanding application pursuant to paragraph 1 OR as a variation of the 2001 agreement, under paragraph 10 and the same test would be applied as to needs of Mark and sufficiency of provision for him. **Therefore, the Court was willing to reopen the agreement and make substantially different provision as it said the agreement did not provide sufficiently for the child's needs.**

Secondly Stephen argued that the judge had erred in imposing financial obligations on Stephen which had the effect of conferring a benefit on Mary, the other child who was not his child, and thus relieving Mary's father of his financial responsibilities. **The court was satisfied that part of the responsibility for Janet's overall debt of £97,000 rested with Mary's father as the debts largely resulted from the costs of moving to a bigger home which was driven by Mary's needs as much as Mark's.** Therefore, the lump sum award should be reduced. **Accordingly the lump sum award to defray Janet's debts was reduced from £100K to £50,000.**

This case has had some rather contentious commentaries from various detractors. It is perhaps difficult to understand why logically Janet's debts from moving from the cottage into the new build estate house were accrued for the benefit of both of the children whereas the lump sum she was awarded from Stephen for the new extensive detached rural housing with stabling was not also for the benefit of both children. However, the principle is an important one: the monies paid must be for the benefit of the child in question, not other children in the family.

It can be a difficult case where the applicant resident carer has gone on to have more children and so cannot work more due to someone else's baby. That might not be the respondent's responsibility but the court is not going to find that the applicant can work more when they can't.

CHAPTER NINE

NEEDS AND AFFORDABILITY

There are two elements to a Schedule 1 claim:

(i) what are the child(ren)'s reasonable needs; and

(ii) what can the payer afford.

It bears repetition that the Act requires the Court at paragraph 4 to consider the following:

Matters to which court is to have regard in making orders for financial relief

"4(1) In deciding whether to exercise its powers under paragraph 1 or 2, and if so in what manner, the court shall have regard to all the circumstances including—

(a) the income, earning capacity, property and other financial resources which each person mentioned in sub-paragraph (4) has or is likely to have in the foreseeable future;

(b) the financial needs, obligations and responsibilities which each person mentioned in sub-paragraph (4) has or is likely to have in the foreseeable future;

(c) the financial needs of the child;

(d) the income, earning capacity (if any), property and other financial resources of the child;

(e) any physical or mental disability of the child;

(f) the manner in which the child was being, or was expected to be, educated or trained.

(2) In deciding whether to exercise its powers under paragraph 1 against a person who is not the mother or father of the child, and if so in what manner, the court shall in addition have regard to—

(a) whether that person had assumed responsibility for the maintenance of the child and, if so, the extent to which and basis on which he assumed that responsibility and the length of the period during which he met that responsibility;

(b) whether he did so knowing that the child was not his child;

(c) the liability of any other person to maintain the child.

(3) Where the court makes an order under paragraph 1 against a person who is not the father of the child, it shall record in the order that the order is made on the basis that the person against whom the order is made is not the child's father.

(4) The persons mentioned in sub-paragraph (1) are—

(a) in relation to a decision whether to exercise its powers under paragraph 1, any parent of the child;

(b) in relation to a decision whether to exercise its powers under paragraph 2, the mother and father of the child;

(c) the applicant for the order;

(d) any other person in whose favour the court proposes to make the order.

(5) In the case of a child who has a parent by virtue of section 42 or 43 of the Human Fertilisation and Embryology Act 2008, any reference in sub-paragraph (2), (3) or (4) to the child's father is a

> *reference to the woman who is a parent of the child by virtue of that section."*

The original seminal case was *Re P (Child: Financial Provision) [2003] EWCA Civ 837.*

This is one of the most notable authorities in the Schedule 1 pantheon on the exercise of discretion. It gives clear guidelines and encapsulates many of the fundamental tenets of this jurisdiction.

There was a two-year old child L born during a four-year relationship. The respondent father was *'fabulously rich'* and ran the "*millionaire's defence*" which is "*whatever you order, I have the resources to pay, so I don't have to disclose my wealth*". This is now just regarded as a case of failure to comply with the rules of disclosure.

The main contested issue was whether it was reasonable to claim that the child's needs were to be met by him providing a fully furnished central London home, a luxury car, an upfront lump sum for school fees and maintenance payments in excess of £100,000 pa. The initial award was rather modest and so the case was taken on appeal. The award made on appeal was as follows:

- £1 million for the purchase of a settled property to return to father;

- £100,000 for internal redecoration;

- periodical payments of £70,000 pa.

This was a considerable increase from the first instance award and it was a 2003 case, when £1m went further with London property than today. The Court of Appeal had regard to the scale of the father's wealth and his chosen way of life. They took the opportunity to set out some guiding principles for Schedule 1 cases which remain good law today:

- the child's welfare, although not paramount, is a *'very relevant consideration'*;

- the length and nature of the parents' relationship, and whether the child was planned, are generally irrelevant;

- the child's financial needs encompass the needs of the caring parent, however, the court should be on guard to ward off unreasonable claims by a parent with the intention of providing for their own benefit;

- where resources permit, the applicant carer will usually require suitable accommodation, settled during the child's minority, a capital allowance for setting up and a car, together with income provision and school fees;

- the overall result should be fair;

- the spending requirements of the parent with primary care should be measured against the social and financial standing of the other parent. For this reason, detailed analysis of budgets will often be counter-productive, although cross-checks should be made from time to time against the raw data of actual spending patterns:

> *'the court must recognize the responsibility, and often the sacrifice, of the unmarried parent (generally the mother) who is to be the primary carer for the child, perhaps the exclusive carer if the absent parent dissociates from the child. In order to discharge that responsibility the carer must have control of a budget that reflects her position and the position of the father, both social and financial.'*

J v C (Child: Financial Provision) [1999] 1 FLR 152 and Re C (Financial Provision) [2007] 2 FLR 13

The child's welfare is "*a constant influence on the discretionary outcome.*"

Now we have the recent case of *Y v Z [2024] EWFC 4,* a very helpful judgment of Peel J, head of the financial remedy courts. He has taken to summarising the law in various areas within seminal judgments and here he gives us his hot-take on Schedule 1.

The background is that the children were aged 2 and 4 years old. Their mother was a world class equestrian, American by birth. She now had poor mental health and within children proceedings had agreed to a 12-18 month psychiatric treatment programme which was progressing. She was found to be anxious and prone to hyperbole. She was the children's primary carer. The father was a cousin of a Middle Eastern ruler but his title was honorific and he took no part in governing or politics and had lived most of his adult life outside of his country of birth. He also had anxiety but to a lesser extent. He was very wealthy. Both parties were found to be trying to tell the truth but their perceptions differed significantly.

They had what was described as a modest family home given the father's wealth: worth £2.3–2.4m in South East England. Their lifestyle was far more luxurious, characterised by private jets or first-class commercial flights, staff, luxury cars and glamorous holidays most months of the year: they had spent £100K on one week's skiing holiday. There were also extensive and expensive horse related purchases and activities. Their personal expenditure was found to be around £2m pa.

In October 2022 the mother and children relocated to the USA. Father was not intending to have any contact with the children.

An interim order was made for £30K pcm periodical payments and whilst M and children were in the UK for various other outgoings at the UK property.

The father ran a millionaire's defence and the Judge said:

> 28. *"Where the millionaire's defence is relied upon, it is customary, in my experience, for at least some disclosure to be provided. There is*

only one reported case which I am aware of where no disclosure at all was required; that was the truly exceptional case of ***HRH Haya bint al Hussein v HH Mohammed bin Rasjid Al Maktoum [2022] 2 FLR 1185****. The facts and circumstances were unique, and that case should not dictate a general approach when a party relies upon the millionaire's defence.*

29. Even when the millionaire's defence is advanced, provision of some disclosure is, in my judgment, usually necessary for the following reasons:

i) It enables the claimant party, and the court, to have some understanding of the scale of wealth and how it is structured, consistent with the requirement on the court (whether under the Matrimonial Causes Act 1973, the Matrimonial and Family Proceedings Act 1984, or Schedule 1 of the Children Act 1989 as the case may be), to consider the income, earning capacity, property and other financial resources of the parties.

ii) It enables thought to be given to the structure and enforceability of any award.

iii) As Macur LJ said at para 21 of ***Re A (A Child: Financial Provision)*** *[2014] EWCA Civ 1577, the extent of wealth "may still inform the reasonableness of the budgetary claims".*

In this case Peel J ordered the Father to provide a Form E but released him from the obligation of disclosure with it but he was required to give a full narrative explanation of the non-standard assets. Peel J permitted the mother to raise a limited number of questions upon that Form E.

He found Mother had some expensive jewellery but little else to her name and might earn up to $60K pa in time. Father declared £111m in capital assets with a significant minority discount applied to his shareholdings and an income of £5.15m pa.

At paragraph 35 Peel J gives us his potted Schedule 1, preproduced here with my highlighting:

> *35. "I have been referred to a number of authorities. From these I draw the following principles:*
>
> *i) The* ***main orders*** *which Schedule 1 entitles me to make are:*
>
> *a.* ***Settlement of property,*** *which invariably will be on a trust, licence or lease arrangement such that the payer retains ownership thereof, and the payee is entitled to occupy with the children during their minority, or until conclusion of tertiary education;* ***Re A*** *[2015] 2 FLR 625 and* ***UD v DN*** *[2021] EWCA Civ 1947.*
>
> ***b. Lump sum or sums for the likes of furniture, car, and clearing debts.***
>
> *c.* ***Child maintenance*** *(secured or unsecured).*
>
> *ii) Each such order, by the wording of the statute must be "****for the benefit of the child****", or made direct to the child (which will be very rare).*
>
> *iii) The court shall have regard to the matters set out at* ***para 4 of Schedule 1 in*** *the exercise of its discretion.*
>
> *iv) Although para 4 does not expressly refer to the welfare of the child, in the generality of cases* ***welfare will be a constant influence*** *on the discretionary outcome;* ***Re P*** *[2003] EWCA Civ 837 at para 44.*
>
> *v) Nor does para 4 refer expressly to* ***standard of living, although in my judgment that is likely to be a highly material factor in many cases, particularly those which fall into the so-called "big money" category.***

vi) In ***Al Maktoum (supra)*** *at para 91, Moor J suggested that "...the children should be able to have a lifestyle that is not entirely out of kilter with that enjoyed by them in Dubia and that enjoyed by [the father] and his family". In* ***Collardeau-Fuchs v Fuchs*** *[2022] EWFC 135 at para 119, Mostyn J observed that standard of living before breakdown of the relationship "...should not however be allowed to dominate the picture as there will be many children, particularly children dealt with under Sch 1, who will not have experienced a standard of living within a functioning relationship either because the liaison between the parents was very brief, or because the child was born after the relationship had come to an end". In my judgment* ***the relevance of the standard of living during the relationship, and the standard of living of each party after the end of the relationship, will vary from case to case,*** *and, as was said at para 21 of* ***Re A (supra), will have to be seen in context***[23].

vii) The court will ordinarily determine the claims in sequence as to (a) property, (b) lump sum or sums, and (c) child maintenance; Re P (supra) *at para 45.*

viii) The court deals with ***property first*** *because, as stated at para 22 of* ***Re A (supra),*** *"The nature of the child's home environment provides the obvious base line from which to consider commensurate levels of maintenance and is as good as any other".*

ix) ***Child maintenance can be interpreted sufficiently broadly to include elements referable to the claimant in his/her capacity as the child's carer; Re P (supra)*** *at paras 48-49. For many years this*

23 In FG v MBW [2011] EWHC 1729 Charles J took the standard of living as subjective and what was enjoyed during the relationship and in the past and future. In H v C [2009] EWHC 1527 HHJ Barnett QC held it was wholly reasonable to aspire to a standard which reflected the father's wealth, or had some relationship to it, even though they had never cohabited and the children had not experienced that.

proposition, or concept, was known as the carer's allowance. More recently, at para 129 of ***Fuchs (supra)*** *Mostyn J has suggested referring to it as a Household Expenditure Child Support Award [HECSA]. Whatever terminology is applied, the principle is clear, although its application is highly discretionary.* ***It is not always easy to draw a bright line*** *between budgetary items to which the claimant has no entitlement as being exclusively personal to him/her, and personal items which may reasonably be claimed as being necessary to discharge the carer's duties, including items which help sustain the carer's physical/emotional welfare;* ***Re P (supra)*** *at para 81.* ***The court "... has to guard against unreasonable claims made on the child's behalf but with the disguised element of providing for the mother's benefit rather than for the child"; J v C (supra)*** *at 159H.*

*x) The court should "****not generally attach weight to the risk that the father may reduce or withdraw his support when the child comes of age*** *(or ceases education or training) thereby obliging the child to adapt to a lower lifestyle at that time";* ***Re P (supra)*** *at para 77(iii).*

xi) In general (and particularly in the bigger money cases), the court is ***entitled to paint with a broad brush*** *and will not ordinarily need to descend into a line-by-line budgetary analysis;* ***Re P (supra)*** *at para 77(i) and* ***Fuchs (supra)*** *at para 129(f).*

*xii) Ultimately, "****the overall result... should be fair, just and reasonable taking into account all of the circumstances****"; Re P* ***(supra)*** *at para 76(viii).*

Peel J set out the structure of the property award at paragraph 50:

"In terms of structure, I suggest as follows, in the knowledge that I did not hear detailed submissions, and precise details will need to be worked out:

i) F should buy the property in his personal name (not the name of a company).

ii) M should have an irrevocable lease for the children's minority (including to the end of tertiary education).

iii) F should undertake not to bring possession proceedings without permission of the English court.

iv) F should pay for structural and external repairs, and M should pay for internal repairs.

v) F should be responsible for buildings insurance, M for contents insurance.

vi) M shall be responsible for all running costs, including homeowner association fees and property taxes.

vii) M may move twice to another property of no greater value than the prior one. F shall pay the costs of the first move, M the costs of the second move.

Here is the judgment with the parents open offers in the same table:

	Mother	**Father**	**Judge**
Value of Housing: settlement and M occupies under a lease	$5.5m	$4m	$5m
Refurbishing/ furnishing	$400K	£700,000 lump sum to include moving costs and security to reduce by each pound paid post offer incl. LSPO	£600,000 to include horses (£90K), debts (£170K), security at the US house (£18), shipping pets (£61K), refurbishment (£250K) No conditions attached to payment
Moving costs incl. pets	£61,872 from UK to US	See above	See above, as M's case
Security for the home	$22,575	See above	See above, as M's case.
2 cars (incl. Nanny)	$150,000 every 4 yrs	$150,000 every 5 years	Accepted F's case
Backdated PPS	£602,400	£0	Refused: for pre Form A maintenance

Child PPS	$780,000 pa	$480,000 pa	$500,000 pa + US CPI indexing
School and Uni fees	Paid by F	Agreed	M to pay uniform, trips, school meals. F to pay Arabic school fees direct.
Horse costs pa	$133,860	£0	No extra

F was ordered to take out life insurance to cover the above costs.

Application for security for payments adjourned but F to deposit £250K for W's legal fees if he defaults.

Interim order for periodical payments to continue until purchase of the property in USA.

CHAPTER TEN

SCHEDULE 1 OUTSIDE OF THE COURT PROCESS

Schedule 1 claims are very susceptible to Non-Court Dispute Resolution (NCDR). They often involve claims for trusts of land as well as Schedule 1, and can be legally complex to run as litigation. There may be a plethora of smaller needs which cannot be agreed, and are not cost effective to litigate. Here I consider a variety of alternative methods of resolving the dispute and some of the pros and cons of the various methods.

An application under the Children Act 1989, Schedule 1 comes under the definition of "*financial remedy*" under Family Proceedings Rules 2010 rule 2.3. Applicants are therefore required under Practice Direction 3A (Family Proceedings Rules 2010) to attend a mediation information and assessment meeting (MIAM) before making the application. This is subject to the usual exemptions which can be found at rule 3.8 of the FPR 2010.

Under the new FPR 2010 R 3 paragraphs 3.3 and 3.4 the court has to consider NCDR and the parties have to file an FM5 form at Court as to their approach to NCDR and what NCDR they have attempted.

The Court can adjourn for NCDR at any stage, it has to consider whether to do so at every hearing, and can adjourn the case for this reason even if the parties do not consent.

Mediation

Draw backs of mediation in Schedule 1 cases:

- The mediator and parties have to have an understanding of the scope of the legislation so that any agreement can be translated into an order; Mediators are often lawyers but often not; if you can find one who is trained, hire a mediator who has expertise in trusts of land and/or Schedule 1;

- Mediation can only be voluntary, so if one side will not agree, or refuses to stand by an agreement which is not yet signed, it cannot take place;

- If a party seeks to resile from a signed mediation agreement the other party has to issue proceedings and an application for a Notice to Show Cause as to why the agreement should not be embodied into an order as a post separation agreement; this can take time and several hearings;

- The parties need to be able to negotiate on a sufficiently level playing field: the quality of the mediator can assist enormously in levelling that field but ultimately if the dynamics are not conducive to a fair mediation it will be a stand-off or a test of who cracks first, rather than a considered resolution of a dispute;

- Particularly, if there has been domestic abuse including controlling or coercive behaviour between the parties, mediation between them alone, in the same room, may not be appropriate as the victim may feel bound to consent, fearful of the consequences of objecting or standing their ground;

- You could consider shuttle mediation, and/ or mediation with lawyers present: the clients sit in different rooms with or without lawyers, and the mediator shuttles between the two sides but if the dynamics are affected by domestic abuse then lawyers or not, mediation is probably not going to be fair;

- Mediation is also not suitable if there are disclosure issues, one party refusing to give information about their relevant assets and income; this has to be compelled by the Court;

- The point of mediation is that the mediator helps the parties to finds a solution acceptable to both. The Court may have imposed something different, but mediation is driven by what the parties will agree. You have to have clients who are realistic in what can be ordered and what is fair.

Benefits of Mediation in Schedule 1 cases:

- There is public funding available for mediation at least for a MIAM and the first £500;

- The court process can feel as drawn out and contentious as an ancillary relief process and mediation is far quicker and more collaborative; it can preserve the relationship of two parties who will remain the parents of their child(ren) forever;

- The court process will be far more costly than mediation, especially if lawyers are involved and even more so if there are trusts of land issues to run alongside Schedule 1;

- Approximately 70% of the financial cases mediated achieve agreement on some issues, so it has a high success rate;

- There are no rules, so mediation can include extended numbers, maybe a relative who is providing financial family support (such as money towards a property), the wealthy parents of a non-resident parent, or older children, perhaps who need support in tertiary education years, or a new partner if the dynamics work;

if the children are younger then the mediator should be trained to mediate with them; running a trial with more than one party and 3 sets of legal fees and/or an older child can be terrifyingly expensive and emotionally dangerous;

- If you need to involve older children, there is child inclusive mediation which is gaining traction as an option but be careful not to put a child in the middle of a conflict: a properly trained and professional child centred mediator will not do this and be aware of the pitfalls:

- Mediation can be used in conjunction with other NCDR or Court methods: maybe to agree the house contents, or ongoing extra payments such as extra-curricular activities and uniform or child arrangements after a Court order on Schedule 1 or to revisit matters which need varying, or to start or finish the NCDR process;

- Mediation can be used at any stage of the process: after an FDR may be a good time, if there is a long delay until a complex and expensive trial, as at that stage each party has heard what one Judge might order and that may have managed expectations. In Schedule 1 your trial may well comprise trusts and land issues as well, so leading to a more complex civil and family hybrid trial, or at the beginning to flush out parties desires, fears and aspirations and explore options.

The Family Mediation Council and its Standards Board has a code of practice, manages registration and handles complaints.

Arbitration

Arbitration is the only binding form of NCDR. The parties sign as ARB1 and delegate decision making to the arbitrator. The decision is then drafted up into a court order which is approved by the Court and is enforced as any court order would be enforced.

The appeal process against an arbitration order is now very similar to that of an appeal from a first instance decision[24]: to a higher court and on the basis that the judgment was wrong in law or no reasonable Judge could have made that decision on that evidence, or the process was sufficiently flawed the result was potentially unfair.

http://ifla.org.uk/divi/wp-content/uploads/Arbitrators.pdf sets out the rules and procedure which are usually used in an arbitration. The arbitrator's authority derives from the Arbitration Act 1996, the Rules, and the agreement to arbitrate.

Arbitrators need to have been trained according to the IFLA rules.

The parties may or may not have commenced litigation when they refer their dispute to arbitration. I have seen both referrals before and during litigation.

I have professional experience of the following benefits of arbitration which would transfer to Schedule 1 cases:

- **A flexible process:** I have seen evidence taken in tranches, or with significant special measures including a client who could only speak with an eye gaze machine, directions hearings held by telephone or by video at 8am to work around everyone's availability; for Schedule 1 there may be a number of smaller needs, such as lump sums for activities for the child or a new car which would be susceptible to this approach and which may get lost in the wash in a formal FDR at Court, but which can be dealt with in arbitration;

---

24 *Haley v Haley* [20201 EWCA Civ 1369, [20211 1 FLR 1429

- In another case I had, the arbitrator wanted the company accountant to answer a variety of questions he had arising from the oral evidence of the business owner; this was done by letter, dictated by the arbitrator after the evidence, and answered and replies distributed before counsel exchanged and filed written closing arguments; this gave the arbitrator a better understanding of the corporate issues and possible resolutions available, even ones counsel had not considered or argued before closing, and the tax consequences of each;

- I have experienced in several arbitrations senior counsel instructed as the arbitrator sharing their experience before the hearing, so they may ask, by email before the hearing, or on one occasion in a telephone directions hearing, for certain cases which they think might be relevant to be addressed at trial;

- Arbitrations are often conducted like trials, but they can be conducted in writing, over the telephone or even on paper as a written exercise;

- **One or all issues**: like with mediation the parties can control what is arbitrated, which may assist if, say, some issues are liable to mediation or have been agreed, but one or two remain;

- **Availability dates:** Cases being listed for full hearings to suit counsel, arbitrator, solicitors and clients, often within 3-4 months of seeking a date and every hearing can be arranged for the availability of everyone, this saves parties having to change advocate so saves on costs;

- **Speed of listing** Directions hearing can take place within a few days of an issue arising; I have had directions listed within less than 48 hours of an issue arising in the week before trial, early morning and by telephone, for everyone's availability;

- **Creative use of time:** When a trial had to be adjourned days before it started, due to late service of professional evidence, the parties used the first day of that booking to instead hold a trial on a preliminary issues (in that case, a cohabitation date, as there were arguments about pre-marital acquest);

- we booked another arbitration hearing around the flights and availability of a litigant who could only enter the country for 90 midnights each year for tax reasons;

- you can control your own process in arbitration so video attendance, if a party lives away or has mobility issues or ill health, is not problematic;

- **Catering for litigants with different needs**: one of my clients came to a hearing with carers, in one arbitration we had a party who had to attend on the telephone as he was confined to bed by his health. I can easily imagine an anxious, older or neuro-atypical party who may need extra breaks, low lights or noise levels or other assistance to engage fully and more confidently in the proceedings and this can be far better catered for and accommodated within an arbitration process where the parties decide where, how and when to conduct the hearing;

- **Qualities of the tribunal**: this is not meant to be a side swipe at any district judge, however, we all know that some cases have unusual features, some are very factually detailed, some have a plethora of legal issues, some of which can be arcane or cutting edge, some cases have parties who need sympathy; some cases would benefit from a particularly calm and constructive tribunal; in arbitration you can choose a Judge who has no links to either party or their advisers or advocates and who may have the necessary expertise and most suitable traits: if you have a case where Schedule 1 is centre stage, you can find an arbitrator with a particular expertise in Schedule 1, maybe also with trusts of land experience, to meet the needs of the case;

- **The time afforded to the Arbitrator for preparation**: an arbitrator who is being paid for the hearing, as counsel would be paid for a hearing, has as much time as it takes to read the documents in the detail needed. However brilliant and experienced they may be, not every Judge is blessed with a list which provides time for that in every case; your arbitrator will have far more time to devote to the parties case, reading the papers and considering the law in the days before the hearing, than a district judge who comes in to 5 cases every day in a busy financial remedy list; that can be very helpful in an area which is not litigated on a daily basis;

- **The owning of proceedings:** both parties agree to arbitration, sign up to it and pay for it; I have too often had a respondent in a case tell me they feel they are being controlled by an applicant who has "made them" come to court when they never wanted to do so, but both agreeing and paying for an arbitrator feels far more equal;

- **Confidentiality:** you can imagine how the local obstetric consultant, family lawyer, Judge, police officer or teacher doesn't really want to sit in the local family court waiting room being recognised by others whom they usually meet in their professional lives. Arbitration can happen far away from Courts and is still wholly confidential;

- **Consistency:** you have the same tribunal for directions and hearing which can be helpful;

- **Written Award:** the arbitrator is obliged to provide a written judgment after any substantive hearing (not directions hearings). This is very helpful to parties and the reasoning is always better when not given ex tempore, or off the cuff, especially where an award may need to be revisited in the future or there are complexities of trusts of land and Schedule 1;

- The arbitrator is discharged once the written award is sent out: you cannot go back to them again.

The arbitration process often intimidates practitioners but in fact the process required is not complicated and is really an easy, more relaxed version of the court process.

- **Choose your arbitrator**; if you cannot agree one then you can ask the IFLA to appoint one for you, but they might not have any particular expertise in your area;

- The **parties submit** to the IFLA Administrator **a Form ARB1FS** (in the case of financial disputes) or Form ARB1CS (in the case of children disputes) signed by both parties in which they describe and define the scope of the dispute they agree to arbitrate.

  The preferred way to submit an ARB1FS or ARB1CS is by email to info@ifla.org.uk.

- These ARB 1 forms need to be **signed by the parties** at the start of the process and once that is done, the parties are now engaged in the arbitration process and the arbitrator is requested to accept the appointment;

- There is a **standard form order** filed at Court to adjourn any extant proceedings pending arbitration; this can be found in the standard form order templates;

- The family **arbitrator contacts the parties** seeking their agreement to the terms of the appointment;

- All correspondence between the family arbitrator and one party must be copied to the other party: **there can be no single correspondence;**

- On agreeing terms, the family arbitrator sends to the parties a **formal letter of acceptance**, whereupon the family arbitration is deemed to have commenced;

- The **normal IFLA rules process** or an alternative agreed process can be used;

- There is usually a **case management hearing,** of some sort, where agreed directions are made, or imposed if that is part of the scope of the arbitration;

- There is usually an **agreed bundle of documents** for the mediator and advocates to use;

- Family arbitration is distinct from mediation in that a decision on the substance of the dispute between the parties is either agreed, sometimes at the door of the arbitration or is **imposed by the family arbitrator** or arbitral tribunal. It is therefore **binding upon the parties** to the dispute;

- The parties have **the right to appeal to court** on a point of law (unless the parties have agreed to exclude this right);

- The parties can also invite the court to **set aside** the award if there has been a serious irregularity which has resulted or may result in substantial injustice;

- In a financial remedy or children family arbitration there will normally be a requirement to **convert the award into a court order** and that is likely to be the case for Schedule 1 as well. Follow the procedure set out in the middle of *S v S [2014] EWHC*

7 (Fam) (and DB v DLJ 2016 EWHC 324 (Fam)), I often send in a copy of the judgment, highlighted at paragraphs twenty three and twenty four, to explain the process to whoever is wading through the box work that day[25];

- Once a court order has been made it may then be **enforced in the usual way** as any other order;

- If the family arbitration involves a civil claim (for example, under TLATA 1996, which is often found in conjunction to Schedule 1 cases) then the parties may apply to court for permission to enforce the award as though it were itself a court judgment or order;

- The costs of the arbitrator, any experts and venue hire are usually shared equally.

Early Neutral Evaluations

These are sometimes called private Financial Dispute Resolutions or "pFDRs" although I tend to agree with the train of thought on legal twitter that this gives an impression of a more expensive fast lane, when in fact it is often faster but usually cheaper, saving the costs of another 6 months of correspondence and another round of updating disclosure, and the expense of slavish compliance with court rules.

An ENE /pFDR is where any senior lawyer, without the need for any particular training, sometimes even a retired Judge, or a deputy district judge, is hired to give a view, a little like a Single Joint Expert. Again, the

25 *BC v BG 2019 EWFC 7* is a case where a party failed to dissuade the Court from over-turning an arbitral award but do read it with *Haley v Haley [20202] EWCA Civ 1369* if you are interested in the procedure and grounds of appeals.

process is flexible, and delays or inconvenient listings are therefore avoided.

It is confidential and personalised.

There is a Private FDR Guide of best practice on the judiciary website.

Those willing to engage in pFDR can find a list on the Financial Remedies Journal website.

Many of the benefits of arbitration are valid here, such as the quality of the tribunal, chance to choose an expert, the time they have to prepare and devote to the parties, who may return several times in a day to the evaluator with different issues as to contents, drafting or timing.

Most ENEs/pFDRs are now run as Court style FDRs, with little practical difference save for looser adherence to the usual rules as to service/filing, bundles and notes.

If you have a pFDR, then the Court does not make the parties go through a Court based FDR as well: the pFDR stands in its stead.

Most chambers who host, have screens and provision for special measures. Tea and coffee and often lunch are all provided on the day.

However, as with an FDR, the indication is not binding, there are not usually directions hearings, the tribunal is not trained in a particular way and there is no written judgment unless your tribunal decides to provide one (which some do now).

If the case does not settle at pFDR or mediation, then you go back into the Court system with a directions/mention hearing. Any hearing of 3 days or more should have a Pre-Trial Review to get it ready for trial.

Any of the above can be mixed up and used in tandem although an arbitrator cannot hop into pFDR or mediator mode if they have an agreed arbitration scope.

Non-Court Dispute Resolution should be the first choice for resolution of most Schedule 1 cases as long as the dynamics allow it to be fair and the parties show a sufficient degree of compliance with disclosure. If they do not, you may want to start the court process and once disclosure is sufficiently complete, move out of court into NCDR.

CHAPTER ELEVEN

SCHEDULE 1 INSIDE THE COURT PROCESS

This section considers the forms which need to be completed for the court process.

Family Proceedings Rules 2010 rule 9.9B sets out that Schedule 1 claims are issued pursuant to the fast track procedure set out in Part 9. It is supposed to be a shorter process and focus on what the parties have now, their income and outgoing needs rather than assets such as pensions. The system is very similar to a variation application procedure in ancillary relief. There are in Schedule 1, no such concepts of marital and pre-marital acquest or contribution. It is purely focussed upon identifying and meeting the need of the children) in a fair and affordable way.

In practice, this means:

Procedure

- This is very like financial remedy;
- A MIAM will be required in the normal way and the forms are the same or similar, so need to be signed off by the mediator;
- Applications are made in Form A1, which is a slightly different Form A[26], the issue fee is currently £303;

---

[26] FPR 2010 PD 5A

- If your case will need more time, then do not hesitate to tick the complex box at Gatekeeping and Allocation stage in the Questionnaire: you will have a 60-minute First Appointment, rather than 45 minutes and 90 minutes for FDR rather than 60 minutes;

- An FM5 needs to be filed which sets out each party's approach to NCDR and the NCDR they have tried and are willing to try;

- It is good practice to comply with the Efficient Conduct Statement as these are financial proceedings under the FPR 2010, even though the statement itself only refers to financial remedy cases and does not list Schedule 1 in the short form procedure;

- Family Proceedings Rules 2010 Part 9 sets out the steps leading up to a first directions hearing and then the FDR appointment;

- The parties can request the longer Form E to be used and longer procedure and the Court will decide whether to accede to that request on paper when listing the first hearing; you can tell from the directions listing which form is required and so which procedural channel is to be used; but the default position is that Form E1 should be used unless a party requests form E and the court agrees FPR 2010 r 9.18 (A1)(a)(iii);

- A First Appointment (FA) will be listed 6–10 weeks after the claim is issued for a short form E1, unless it agrees on request to move to the longer form procedure when it will be 12–16 weeks before the FA is listed;

- Within 4 days of issue the Court should serve a copy of the application a notice of the hearing and blank E1 on the respondent(s) which will include the date for the parties to exchange form E(1) and preliminary documents;

- If the other side is not ready, send your form to the court and await the other side, so you can exchange forms with each other at the same time but you are not late with your court filing date; the date for filing and exchanging will be on your directions order from the court;

- If you want to use the short form procedure and serve an agreed set of directions, there is provision for that;

- If you are using the longer-term procedure then it is 35 days before your FA that the Forms E1 should be filed and exchanged, and then 14 days before that hearing the questionnaire is due and the day before the chronology, ES1, and ES2;

- Remember, a questionnaire should be no more than 4 pages long (Efficient Conduct Statement);

- The Court can convert the FA into a Financial Dispute Resolution hearing in the usual way, if both parties agree, and the Court is notified in advance; the procedure should feel very familiar, save for the modified forms;

- The Court can, under para 9, make interim orders for periodical payments at the FA and the Act allows interim periodical payment orders. However, experience shows that district judges with a busy list are reluctant to do so unless there is a clear ability to pay and there is some notice to the other side so they are not taken by surprise;

- There is no commitment to provide judicial continuity with the short form procedure, although in practice in most provincial or smaller courts there will be little difference from the usual case list;

- There is a Schedule 1 order precedent at 2.2 under the standard financial and enforcement orders.

Adding Parties at the First Appointment

You may wish to consider joining an older child as a co-applicant, maybe one who is seeking support for tertiary education. It is obviously far better to do this before issue, but it can be done at the FA.

You may wish to join third parties who have an interest in say a property, maybe grandparents who have contributed and declare a beneficial interest.

Joinder is pursuant to the rules at FPR 2010 R 9.26B.

The potential intervenors should be served with Form A(1) before the FA if possible. If they have not been, then you can serve them after the hearing. They should be invited to consider whether they wish to intervene in the proceedings. They are unlikely to be compelled to do so. It is not a step to take lightly as there are costs implications for a third set of legal fees. If the third parties make a claim to some/ any of the assets in issue and they are successful, then it is likely their costs will be paid by the party who denied their claim, or by both parties and then apportioned between them[27] as FPR 2010 R 28.3 does not apply to intervenors and their costs usually follow the event.

Once an intervenor has been joined to the proceedings, the guidance in *TL v ML and Others (Ancillary Relief: Claim Against Assets of Extended Family)* [2005] EWHC 2860 (Fam) should ordinarily be followed:

---

27 *Baker v Rowe 2010 1 FLR 761 cf paragraphs 24 and 25 which suggests costs follow the event*

(i) The third party should be joined to the proceedings at the earliest opportunity;

ii) Directions should be given for the issue to be fully pleaded by points of claim and points of defence;

iii) Separate witness statements should be directed in relation to the dispute; and

iv) The dispute should be directed to be heard separately as a preliminary issue, before the FDR para 36.

My experience is that in many modest asset cases the district judges do not want to put everyone at risk on costs and are reluctant to press the button and join third parties too early in the proceedings although the case law suggests it should be done that way. It may be the difference of approach depending upon the level of assets at stake and proportionality of costs. I have had district judges ask the third-party intervenors to come with representation to an FDR, not allow them to become an intervenor yet, but to approve any settlement. I have also had a judge ask the third party to file a statement or letter setting out their position rather than joining them and filing full statements, and for the parties to then set out their position upon the third-party claim in response to the letter. I have had other cases where we have filed and served full pleadings, or commercial points of claim as to the intervenor claims particularly if there are complex trusts or land issues.

Checklist of useful tips

- Don't forget to use the complex box at gatekeeping and allocation to bag more time at your court hearing; often these cases are complex or have issues such as non-disclosure;

- You can ask for the longer-term procedure when filing and making the application, and the Court will then list it like a financial remedy standard procedure matter;

- The Court can under para 9 make interim orders for periodical payments;

- You should consider whether the child (usually an older child), a grandparent with an interest in the property or any other party needs to be invited to join as a third party at the FA[28];

- The section on trusts of land has some other tips for the first hearing if you are running a joint case of trusts of land and Schedule 1.

Evidence Gathering: Form E(1)

The Form E1 is the central document for the presentation of evidence in most cases. Do read it carefully, and the notes. They answer many of the questions I am often asked.

If there is a good reason why you cannot attach all of the documents required, you can offer to send them on later. Do notify the court and other party of this when you file and serve the form.

This section gives some tips for the less experienced practitioner, or a useful checklist on completion of a Form E(1). I also set out some practice points.

The form is well drafted. So often, delays in cases are caused, and FAs not converted to FDRs because the Form E has not been accurately or fully completed and/or the Efficient Conduct Statement ignored. Many

---

28 R9.26B FPR 2010

questionnaires include questions which are requests for the Form E to be properly completed. Delays can be kept to a minimum, First Appointments more often converted to Financial Dispute Resolution hearings, and costs reduced if the Form E (1) is completed as required from the outset. A Schedule 1 case is often susceptible to an early FDR, but only if the evidence before the Court is sufficient for the Judge to give a clear indication.

Form E headings and layout:

1. General Information
2. Financial Details (assets and liabilities and income)
3. Financial Requirements (outgoings and capital needs)
4. Other Information (narrative boxes, claims for conduct, contribution adjustments and needs)
5. Order Sought

Form E1 headings and layout:

1. General Information
2. Employment
3. Other Income
4. Capital
5. Income Needs
6. Financial Needs of child(ren)

7. Financial Details Summaries.

Example Authority

Even if the other side succeed in their application, if they have not given proper disclosure to allow you to understand their case and make a sensible analysis of it, you might be able to argue for your costs.

Lemmens v Barbara Brouwers (Ex Lemmens) [2018] EWCA Civ 2963:

Party who won case still ordered to pay some costs of other party because he had not given disclosure until the door of the court.

This is a joyous little case of an appeal from Nicholas Cusworth QC about costs and variation of periodical payments in an ancillary relief case. The husband brought a variation application and succeeded in securing a downward variation in payments. However, he had failed to really show his hand and explain his financial position to the wife until the door of the court. The Judge had therefore summarily assessed costs at the end of the hearing and ordered him to pay 25% (£30K) towards the wife's costs because he had not been open and given full and frank disclosure, so she was unable to make a sensible appraisal of the strengths and weaknesses of his case, decide whether his application had merit and make a proper offer to settle.

The guidance given by Peel J in *WC v HC* [2022] EWFC 22 holds good for Schedule 1 cases:

> *"7. Parties, and their legal advisers, may be under the impression that to describe the other party in pejorative terms, and seek to paint an unfavourable picture, will assist their case. It is high time that parties and their lawyers disabuse themselves of this erroneous notion."*

General Information (Forms E and E1)

I have followed the format of the Form E

Parties Occupations

Just be aware that if there is an issue about what the party can earn this may have some importance. I have had a case recently where the description of the financially weaker party's occupation was taken from the marriage certificate and copied into the Form E. It seemed uncontroversial. The party was not yet earning as the child had only started school the week before and this party was the primary carer. Further the parties were still living together. However, she was not in fact qualified as described and so it was an inaccurate description of the party's qualifications. It led to numerous potential job details being filed by the other side, when the difference in income between what she could in fact earn and what she could earn if she were indeed qualified as described was significant. It affected the periodical payments needed and her real mortgage capacity and so what she needed to rehouse. The matter is now going to trial, partly on the party's qualifications and so her earning capacity.

Schedule 1 is all about needs, so provide job adverts for what you say the applicant can do if their earning potential/capacity is in issue. Don't forget this may be a staged process if there is a probationary period and/or qualification, or a civil service career ladder.

Cohabitation/ Living with a partner

In Schedule 1 the length of relationship of the parties is not a factor but it may be relevant to the context of whether or for how long a child became used to living at a certain standard of living. The case of *MB v EB [2019] EWHC 1649 (Fam)* is an authority on the point of defining marital cohabitation, and the point at which separation occurred, given there was scope for debate on the point in the facts of that case, but the better case on cohabitation for Schedule 1 purposes is probably still *McCartney v Mills [2008] EWHC 401 (Fam)*, a judgment of Mr Justice Bennett from paragraphs 55-64 in particular. This is not the cohabitation of the parties together but whether they are now cohabiting with a new partner who has a mortgage capacity and contributes to the household outgoings.

Questionnaire

The Efficient Conduct Statement says this should only be 4 pages long for standard form procedure in financial remedy, so probably should be no longer in the short form procedure.

If your instructions are that the other party is cohabiting, and this is relevant to how much of the outgoings fall to them, or how much is needed to rehouse, then ask the question if it is not referenced. As an alternative, ask where the partner lives if not with the other party. Ask how many nights a week they spend together and if they holiday together. Social media often provides evidence of this or the electoral role, of where someone pays council tax.

One way to check cohabitation is to see if you can identify all of the relevant outgoings from the party's bank statements: all utilities, food bills, mobile telephone, fuel etc. If there are outgoings missing from the bank statements, then ask about it as they may be paid by the partner. Ask about their income, capital base and their mortgage capacity. The payee might be able to raise a lump sum, with a partner behind them, or if a property is sold, to house themselves for less than was thought if there are two of them to be on a new mortgage.

The question has to be tied to a practical and relevant issue. If you are the usual case where the Child Maintenance Service will deal with periodical payments, then none of this may be of any relevance, even if a party is being coy or untruthful, or it might be of relevance to housing need, mortgage capacity or what level of outgoing the payee has to meet and so whether they have income left to manage debts.

Dependants

The Form E1 asks for details of children living with you, not living with you and other dependants. The Form E does not ask about dependants who are not children. These could include older relatives and dependant relatives who have caring needs or who need financial support. Consider a sibling with a stable income who is paying the legal fees of another sibling who is embroiled in their own financial remedy issues: that is a financial dependent. Don't forget children at University who need a bedroom, who might not walk into a job and become self-supporting upon graduation, or who live at home when studying at a local University. There may also be children who live only part of the time at the property, such as step-children or half siblings.

Health: Party

This is really searching for whether a party's health affects their housing need, income capacity or whether it has some other financial effect. Clients often want to list health issues for other reasons. However, if a health issue interferes with employment and so earning capacity, or the stability of earning capacity it may be important. If possible, back this up with a letter from the GP or copies of GP notes, suitably highlighted or redacted, which are cheaper to secure than a full medical report from a consultant. Remember FPR Part 25 states that permission is needed to file expert evidence however, so cover this off in your FA order if possible.

Occupational health reports are rare in Schedule 1 cases as they are so expensive. GP records can usually be secured from the NHS app.

Health: Child

Again, the relevance is usually the effect upon earning capacity or housing needs and the cost of any treatment, support, transport or even the length of time the child will remain at home. Does this interfere with the caring adult's earning capacity due to number of appointments or caring needs? Are there future risks in a condition which may interfere with earning capacity? Are the housing needs directly shaped by the child's condition, such as needing single storey accommodation or wide doorways? Will the child be able to live independently or semi independently? All of these need to be supported by medical evidence, again, copied medical notes and/or a report(s) from GP or consultant, depending upon who is best placed to give an opinion on the point.

I had one child who was found to need extra time after Masters to secure a job as they would need such a level of reasonable adjustment in the work place and so PPS were ordered for a year after graduation.

The child may have one off needs for equipment or tutoring, support groups or transport. A neuro atypical child or one with different learning needs may require special support. The cost of a Masters course may not be available through Student loans. In the case of *MT v OT [2018] EWFC 868 (Fam)* the children had extra learning needs and the Court awarded the resident carer mother a sum to cover tuition fees during the sixth form years. She had provided evidence of the future cost of this expense, and it was held to be a legitimate need.

Costs of education

This can encompass the costs of future university fees, accommodation, travel and living and certainly fees which are not covered by a student loan such as for a Masters after a 4 years course or an expensive Masters, such as the business related ones.

Child maintenance calculation

Use the government website www.gov.uk/calculate-child-maintenance for an accurate calculation. Don't forget about the deduction for pension contributions and other children living in the home of the payer. You should be able to calculate this gross income after pension contributions from payslips and/or the last P60.

If there has been contact with the CMS that is often on the telephone and may need to be evidenced in writing by way of email and this might not be a simple process.

Questionnaire

If you are acting for the receiving party do look out for Additional Voluntary Contributions to pensions, so paying extra into a pension to reduce the child support liability and ask questions to confirm if those are indeed voluntary contributions. Not only can this be tax efficient for the payer but it also for the time being depresses the child support calculation.

Tenure of property in which party lives

Do remember to consider carefully the terms of occupation of the property in which the party is living. Is rent payable? Is there security of tenure? Under a lease a tenant has *exclusive* possession of the property and can exclude the landlord. If it is not a lease, is it a licence with no security? Is the lease at an end? If so under the Assured Shorthold Tenancy terms either landlord or tenant can give notice although there is at the time of typing legislation in the pipeline to provide more protection to tenants. Could the actions of another put the stability of the tenure at risk? Is the rent or mortgage being paid regularly and on time and in full? If it is not, then after 2 months default, it may be that action may be started by the mortgagee or landlord for repossession.

If that is the case, and housing is at risk, do you need to make a claim for interim periodical payments? If there is no security of tenure then that should be made clear on the form.

Do you need a mortgage capacity report if the payee has limited mortgage capacity and/or poor credit rating, even if it is Brief Indicative Material, a short form report, for a FA rather than a full mortgage report for an FDR (see the requirements in the Efficient Conduct Statement).

Financial Details (Form E) / Capital Form E1 Part 4

Real Property

This section on real property is often left incomplete giving rise to delays and questions. Fill it in.

Value

Both forms E/E1 ask for a valuation of the property obtained in the last 6 months. It is only if this CANNOT be obtained that the forms allow for a guesstimate of value by the client. A market appraisal is an estate agent's view of what the property is worth on sale. Make sure it differentiates between sale price and marketing price, though. These are usually free of charge. They could be in an email. The format is not really important. Sometimes going back to the agent who sold the property to the parties can assist, if the party trying to value the property cannot gain access to it. Web based calculators are not terribly accurate and I have yet to meet a Judge who is happy to rely upon them. In extremis a "drive by" valuation can assist a party who cannot gain access, particularly if the property is maybe an estate house or one where there are very similar properties nearby. The value has to be up to date even if there is an argument about work which has been done, or increased value after a particular date.

Don't forget to check for planning applications nearby if there is a risk of that or for Grenfell/cladding issues which engage the Building Safety Act 2002 where properties may be unsaleable or mortgagees may refuse to lend on them.

The **Land Registry title number** is important. The HM Land Registry title documents should highlight what charges are attached to the property. Be aware it can take up to 6 months to update at the moment but searching is not expensive.

If there is **a restriction** registered against a property, maybe by a financially weaker applicant left in a property not registered in their name, then the final order will have to encompass removal of that, which may need to be co-ordinated with a re-mortgage.

The forms require an up-to-date **mortgage redemption statement.** Do look out for:

- are there any early repayment charges (ERCs) and when do those expire;

- if it is an interest only mortgage is there an endowment attached, or an investment vehicle of some sort and importantly when does the capital have to be repaid? these mortgages have a time limit after which the entire capital sum must be repaid;

- how much has been repaid off the capital (if it is a repayment mortgage) and who has paid that? If one party is staying in the house and the other is paying the mortgage how will that work going forward and what effect will that have if any on beneficial ownership?

- can the client who wants to stay in the property secure the release of the other party from the mortgage? If they cannot, then the house may have to be sold or the party who is out will need to be able to raise a mortgage on their own and buy out the other party.

> If a party is cohabiting can they raise another mortgage with their cohabitee or if the person left in the house has a partner can they come on the mortgage and release the other party from their obligations? Parties are often nervous about confessing to having a new partner, thinking of the emotional fallout, but in finance cases it can be very useful as if the issue is sell the house to release capital or buy out, then the new partner's mortgage capacity may unlock a deal.

You need to calculate the costs of sale. The Red Book notes the case of *Behzadi v Behzadi [2009] 2 FLR 649:* in default of evidence to the contrary sale costs should be taken at 3% of the gross sale price. Most Judges are currently accepting 2% - 3% and many cases compromise on 2.5%.

Questionnaire

If you are unsure how many properties the other party owns, ask them to file a PN1 search, which is a trawl of the Land Registry to see what is registered in their name. If they won't agree, then ask for the Court's permission at FA to use their details to do so, that way you will not be in breach of GDPR Art 6.

Mortgage capacity of a party should be evidenced by a mortgage broker letter, not a screenshot from a mobile telephone banking app. You need to know the term of the mortgage offered, is it only a low amount because the party has asked to borrow over a short period of time or a high repayment rate? What did they base their application on? What income did they declare? Ask for the evidence. They may have only given their salary and not dividend take, for example.

Bank accounts

You are required to provide the last 12 months statements for any bank, building society or other account held by the party, or by the party and one other or in which they have an interest but which is not in their name at all.

The second section is the same but for all sorts of investments, including shares. The statements in support are not required, as with bank statements, to be 12-months' worth but an up-to-date statement.

Questionnaire

Do search the internet for a payee you don't recognise and ask if it appears it could be to some form of savings vehicle or support for a partner.

Policies

The most common mistake with these is whether they have a payment out upon death or other event such as critical illness, or whether they have a surrender value, so a savings element.

Belongings

These need to be the actual value, not replacement values taken from a new for old insurance policy. Remember, few judges are going to order sale of the hot tub and push bikes to fund housing so be proportionate. Cars can be downsized, however.

Liabilities

Even cards with a nil balance should be listed.

Debts should be considered in terms of when they may be called in, whether they are soft or hard, or even a gift, especially if they are from family or friends. In *P v Q [2022] EWFC B9* per HHJ Hess paragraph 19 the judge sets out the sort of factors which will determine what is a gift, and what a loan, and whether that loan is going to be considered a repayable debt (hard loan) or repayable at will (soft loan).

Capital Gains Tax

This calculation can be complicated. It is tax on the profit made on a capital asset. It attaches to properties but also shares and any other capital item upon which there is profit. The rates changed in the October 2024 budget: check the rates and use an online calculator for simple assets. For property, particularly where a party seeks to offset works done, this may need extra intervention. There is a relief called principal private residence relief which provides an exemption if the property is the party's home but only for the time pro rata that is has been the person's home with an 18-month buffer. There are other possible deductions to the profit element before different tax bands are then applied. There is a government calculator at www.tax.service.gov.uk for working out the CGT payable on property which has not been lived in as a home by all of the owners throughout the period of ownership. If that is not sufficiently sensitive. then ask an accountant to work it out. The cost is usually modest and attach the letter to the Form E or send it in later with a request/Part 25 application on a D11 at FA for permission to rely upon it. If you can agree it before FA even better, but the decision of whether to allow it to be filed as expert evidence, is for the court, not the parties, so you still have to ask permission to file.

Business assets

The last 2 years of business accounts need to be attached.

This is Schedule 1, not a financial remedy claim. You are likely to be far more interested in the liquidity of the business what money can be released as a cash lump sum, rather than the value of the shares or the precise tax payable upon their disposal. This is an area which can suck up a lot of cost to little or no end, if the lawyer and/or client is not focussed on the real issues. It is unlikely you want the payer to sell their shares or business as that would remove the income stream. These shares may well be an asset available to the other party but how can they assist in the case?

It may be the shares or a company asset can be charged to raise money, especially if the company is owed and run by the payer. If the payer is not sole owner then if they declare a dividend to release monies they will have to pay one to the other shareholders too and dividend income tax.

It may be that a director could take a director's loan from the company but co directors may have to vote on that and if they are not a director then that route is closed without co-operation of others.

If the business is in effect a vehicle for a sole trader then it may only have the value of its assets, cash in the bank and van, maybe some tools and some goodwill. A business such as a hairdressers or coffee shop may have a lease which has some value. Maybe a party can borrow against the lease as security for raising money for a lump sum payment.

Remember to get money out of the business account the party will have to pay income tax or dividend tax on it or they will need to be pulling down a director's loan, which is tax free because it is the return to them of money they have loaned the business. It is often a dividend declared, and for which tax has been paid, but which has not been paid out of the company, as the party has left the money in the bank account. At the end of the year the accountant writes it down in the books as a director's loan. This can be paid out, tax already paid, and there is no need to pay out any other director, as with declaration of dividend and other shareholders.

If the business is a limited company then the shares held by the party are what the court needs to value, even if broadly. If the company is a business for a sole trader then the value of the assets held, including cash, less tax due, and some goodwill may be enough after consideration of capital gains tax, again. A party who owns a high percentage of shares and is an office holder or a sole trader might be entitled to business asset disposal relief. The rates changed in the October 2024 budget for sales after 6th April 2025 (up from 10% to 14%) and changes again for sale after 6th April 2026 (up to 18%).

However, a business with employees, or another director and/or shareholder may well need a formal valuation to resolve any questions about value. If it is a trading company, it might be valued on a multiple of its sustainable profit, taking off debt and removing the cash (which is never sold with the business, save for the minimum necessary for ongoing trade). If it is a company which holds assets, like a property development company, then those may need to be separately valued by a surveyor, before an accountant can value the company on an asset basis. You may have a business which is a hybrid of the two. Any such valuation should be done pursuant to FPR 2010 Part 25, by an accountant, on an SJE basis, although you may need a surveyor to value property held by the company. There are many outfits offering to value companies who are not accountants, but the court will want an accountant to value, if that is relevant.

This is Schedule 1 however, and you are not able to argue entitlement and sharing, but you might be interested in liquidity. You may need an accountant to tell you not what the shares are worth but what the party can extract from the company and the tax payable on that money i.e. liquidity and what a sustainable income might be for the payer. That may be far more pertinent to resolution of the case.

Do look at the Articles of Association for the company, which you can find on the Companies House Beta website for free. They often set out that shares cannot be sold or transferred without the approval of the directors, so making them unsaleable in practice in many circumstances.

Some people attach a valuation of shares from the company accountant, although this may well not be acceptable to the other party.

Questionnaire

- Ask about whether any previous offers have been made for the shares in the company, and if so the terms of the offer and documentary evidence of it;

- Always ask about any shareholder agreements or dividend policies. If you don't trust what you are being told then ask to see the minutes of the meeting which made the decision (which can be suitably redacted if need be, to preserve the details of the others present).It may be that some shares could be transferred to another holder or third party and so release funds, although there will be tax to pay. It may be that a large divided is about to be declared;

- Use Companies House Beta online to look at the other party, the company in question and look for any other companies that may be listed under the party's names, or even their new cohabitee, if they have one. Be aware that the same individual will often have their names spelled differently or put a "Mr/Mrs/Miss/Ms" in front of the name, or change the spelling so that it shows up a different individual so play around with the name. I had one case where the husband set up a new company which was going to do some of the family company business. He listed himself at Companies House with a different spelling of his first name so that the wife would not find him when she searched.

- You are likely to only find micro accounts at Companies House with no Profit and Loss sheet, unless the company is audited. So you may need 2 or 3 years of full statutory (year end) accounts. Look to see when the last set were signed off and you can judge when the next accounts are due.

- You might have a tame accountant who can tell you on an anonymised set of documents if there is any real value in the shares, liquidity issues or point in looking at an SJE.

Pensions

You need to file and serve the last Cash Equivalent Transfer Value pension statement with this section. One is provided every year. It is difficult to see how a pension share might be made as there is no provision to do so under the Schedule, but the parties might agree this if the payer is very much older or maybe there is a grandparent carer; a pension member, if aged 55 years (rising to 57 yrs in 2028) may be able to access a lump sum from their pension (25% tax free) if liquidity is needed to meet a lump sum claim, or in time such a lump sum may be available to repay an interest only mortgage.

Income

I almost never see this page completed fully either, but do try to do so, as it is a central part of any case involving periodical payments and Schedule 1. Completing it fully might save a questionnaire and replies which can delay matters by several months, depending upon listing in your court. Think what you would ask if you were acting for the other party.

It requires a P60, the last 3 payslips and the last P11D which will list taxable perks of the job, and give a value for any medical cover, car allowance or similar provided by the employer.

A figure therefore for last year's **net income is needed,** not turnover, not profit, but income, and an estimate for the next 12 months with an explanation if it is very different from the last year.

When are the next accounts due? Are these going to be very different? Why?

Note your pension contributions and any other expenses. These would be deducted if employed. The final figure again appears to be net of everything, or money in hand.

You might include the ***employment contract and any accompanying documents*** if it defines bonus/commission payments, the terms of share options or any deferred options, and what terms of conditions govern when they are awarded, or a probationary period.

Share options and bonuses are very useful as they might provide lump sums of cash for a Legal Services Payment Order or lump sum payment.

You might include evidence of whether extra hours are available for a part time worker by way of an email from the employer/ HR department.

Explain the ***payslip entries,*** again to save questionnaires:

Are there staff salary sacrifices?

Are there childcare vouchers available? If so, what is the account worth and produce evidence of it; this should probably be included under the "other assets" paragraph a few pages earlier; this is a scheme for saving tax free money to use for childcare and like a Paypal account or similar it might have a residual value if the vouchers are not all used.

What are the pension and any Additional Voluntary Contributions (AVCs) made by the party and their employer?

Do they pay union or other subscriptions and are these compulsory?

Are there any share save or other savings schemes and if so explain the terms and conditions and any residual value.

Net income appears to be net of everything, or what we might call "in hand".

Questionnaire

Ask about expenses entitlements: if the party is employed what were the claims made last year and for what? They might get a large mileage allowance which in effect turns them a small profit or reduces their outgoings. They might get their car fuel, insurance and MoT paid. Ask for the terms and conditions and amount of claims from Human Resources or the employer as confirmation. For a sole trader or director what do they claim as expenses and can the company accountant confirm that. You can look at the profit and loss part of the accounts where expenses are listed but that might not break it down enough for you to discern exact monthly income/outgoings. Ask what have they claimed in the 12 months before these proceedings started when they did not know they were going to be scrutinised?

If a party has a loan (including mortgage) taken out ask to see their application for it as often a party will put their income at its highest on that, because they want the credit, and they are more honest than on their self-assessment tax forms when they are trying to reduce their profits.

Other income

If you are recording rental income, make sure you are clear whether you are recording the net or gross figure of works on the property and expenses including mortgage payments, but also of tax.

Ask the client what they pay tax on, and then what the credits are to their bank statements: banking apps can isolate credits very easily.

This could be family income or an older child paying rent.

Is there income from say solar panels on the house, or expenses for being a local councillor?

Questionnaire

If your client was a co-owner of a rented property but did not deal with the income, remember the income and personal tax is apportioned, so just check that your client is not going to get an unexpected tax bill for rental income which has been apportioned to them as an owner but which they have not received. You need to ask about the income tax position: who has paid what to date and what is outstanding.

Ask about credits into the bank accounts but most of my cases have questionnaire questions wasted because a credit is from another bank account owned by the party and no-one has checked the numbers.

If the party cohabits, ask if the cohabitee provides any money into the household or the parent of another child who lives with the applicant; how do they divide the payment of bills?

Income needs

This and the next box on needs are some of the most important boxes in the form for Schedule 1 claims.

Savings are an acceptable expense for most income levels, as are pensions and life insurance, so if self-employed make provision for these standard benefits of employment.

Don't just copy down what was spent before separation, because there will be not enough money to sustain that into the future.

Questionnaire

This is a common area where cross examination points are listed in challenging outgoings which are set too high. Save the questions for whether an expense exists at all, rather than challenging a figure which may change by a few pounds. Remember that up to FDR the court approach is quite broad brush. A detailed analysis, line by line of a budget, is not going to be undertaken until final hearing (unless you are having an interim Pps hearing or a LSPO hearing) by which time you will have had narrative statements on the detail.

Remember *Re P (Child: Financial Provision) [2003] EWCA Civ 837:* a detailed analysis of budgets will often be counter-productive, although cross-checks should be made from time to time against the raw data of actual spending patterns

Do ask for proof about big numbers if they are disputed.

Don't ask about things your client can check themselves, like what the council tax is for the other party's property.

Do be proportionate and catch yourself on, as the Irish would say, about the optics: don't quibble about the cost of a window cleaner at £15 pcm, when your client has just spent £10K on a skiing holiday.

Capital Needs

Try to attach sample properties to support the level of housing need sought. Calculate the SDLT, or stamp duty and land tax upon purchase. You are probably attaching their mortgage capacity, too, so be realistic about how that dovetails into housing aspiration.

District Judges are often swayed by practical considerations: where are the child(ren)'s schools? Is there a school bus route nearby? How does the primary carer get to work from the proposed housing area, and get the children to school? Where are the parties in relation to each other for child arrangements?

There will be moving costs, refurbishment, curtains and carpets and legal costs if the home is to be sold and new one purchased. There may be furniture if the house furniture is to be split or white goods if they were fitted in a property which is being sold. This may create a lump sum need.

A car and a lump sum to defray debt are also both acceptable.

Standard of Living

This is not listed as a specific consideration in the checklist for Schedule 1 but the standard of living can assist in whether requesting settlement of a house in an expensive area is fair, in light of the standard of living experienced or not by the child and monies available.

Example Authorities

J v C (Child: Financial Provision) [1999] 1 FLR 152

Hale J (later Baroness Hale of the spider brooch) noted that whilst the standard of living enjoyed during the relationship is not a factor set out in Schedule 1, nevertheless the child should be brought up in circumstances which bear some relationship to the Father's.

F v G (Child: Financial Provision)[2005] 1 FLR 261

Singer J noted that the lifestyle which had become the child's normal could impact upon the assessment of the child's needs: *"In some cases… the standard of living enjoyed by child (and mother) during lengthy pre-separation cohabitation… could promote the standard of living so long enjoyed by the child to the position of an important, if not the dominant, feature of the case. Here the …cohabitation lasted far less long, but during their relationship … the parents lived in a way where little expense was spared and generous indulgences were frequent."*

A Mother v A Father (Re Schedule 1 of the Children Act 1989) [2024] EWFC 63 is a recent example of this application of the section. The parents had very different income/ asset positions. F had £ 2.9m in non-pension assets and an income of @£107K pa gross (under the maximum CMS cap: so PPS not available). M had the flat she had bought worth @£380K and no real earnings due to her mental health. The Judge found she could probably earn £16–18K rising to @£25K pa.

The child was 11 years old.

M/child's housing need was put at £475K, for a 2 bed property (may be a flat) near to school, friends and activities. The family home was worth £1.25m.

F therefore to pay M £150K to bridge the gap between £380K in the flat and £475K housing need with SDLT included. The £150K to revert to F on child finishing full time secondary education or attaining 18 yrs whichever was later.

Lump sum of £20K ordered to provide a car.

F agreed to pay school fees and reasonable extras such as extracurricular activities and the wrap around care would allow M more scope to work. Voluntary school trips were to be a shared cost.

A lump sum sought by M for uniform and other expenses was found to be income by another name.

Conduct and contributions

This has been thought to be irrelevant for Schedule 1 until we had the recent case of *TK v LK [2024] EWFC 71* and the judgment of Nicholas Allen KC sitting as a Deputy High Court Judge as set out above. This was the case where the child was now living with F as M had been imprisoned for an offence against the child. F and child were now living in different countrys but M was habitually resident in this jurisdiction. F said that M had inherited from her father (in another jurisdiction) a sum of @£375K. M disagreed and said she did not have access to those sums and had nothing to her name, in effect.

At paragraphs 59-61 of the judgment:

> *"59… It is a consequence of the court's focus on the child's needs and requirements under Schedule 1 rather than those of their parents that* ***conduct is even less likely to be relevant than it may be under MCA 1973*** *(see A v A (A Minor: Financial Provision) [1994] 1 FLR 657 per Ward J (as he then was) at p664 - "Conduct, or more accurately, misconduct, which is not a specific factor in the para 4 checklist as it is in the Matrimonial Causes Act, s 25, checklist, is therefore material only as a hazard light which will flash throughout my journey down the rest of para 4" - and Re S (Unmarried Parents: Financial Provision) [2006] 2 FLR 950 where Bennett J was criticised by the Court of Appeal at [15] for having lost sight of the child's needs due to his focus on the mother's conduct).*
>
> *60.However,* ***it is clear that particularly egregious conduct can be taken into account.*** *For example in O v P (No 2) (Sch 1 Application: Stay: Forum Conveniens) [2015] 2 FLR 77 ……*
>
> ***61. The authorities in relation to conduct under MCA 1973 s25(2)(g) are therefore relevant."***

The Judge found there had been conduct as the M's behaviour was so "egregious" and it had had a financial consequence: F and child had moved to another country to keep themselves safe.

It was also a case where the Judge found that M's non-disclosure and her lack of credibility meant he was able to make findings as to her having assets which she had not declared, using the standard financial remedy case of *Moher v Moher* [2020] 1 FLR 225 paragraph 80-91.A lack of disclosure can lead the Court to draw adverse inferences against a party. In this case M was also lacking credibility in some of her Replies. He found she had @£341K in inheritance.

Under the standard financial remedy cases such as *OG v AG [2021]1 FLR 1105* and more recently in *Tsvetkov v Khayrova* [2023] EWFC 130 per Peel J, conduct is only one of the following and it would be inequitable to disregard it:

(i) conduct with a "gulp factor";

(ii) non-disclosure;

(iii) *Norris* add-backs where there has been wanton and frivolous dissipation of assets;

(iv) litigation misconduct which is usually penalised in costs.

Mr Allen KC continued as to *Tsvetkov*:

> *"63.......At [43] Peel J stated that at 'stage one' a party asserting conduct must prove:*
>
> > *i) the facts relied upon;*
> >
> > *ii) if established, that those facts meet the conduct threshold, which has consistently been set at a high or exceptional level; and*
> >
> > *iii) that there is an identifiable (even if not always easily measurable) negative financial impact upon the parties which has been generated by the alleged wrongdoing. A causative link between act/omission and financial loss is required. Sometimes the loss can be precisely quantified, sometimes it may require a broader evaluation. But I doubt very much that the quantification of loss can or should range beyond the financial consequences caused by the pleaded grounds."*

So conduct is possible to run as an argument BUT:

(i) it will be very rare;

(ii) it is limited to one of the four scenarios from *OG v AG above*;

(iii) it must be inequitable to disregard it;

(iv) it must be properly pleaded at the earliest opportunity in accordance with *Tsvetkov;*

(v) the current authority states that it must have a financial effect.

<u>**Other party's income and assets**</u>

This does need to be filled in fully.

Questionnaire

I have had a case where monies were transferred into an account which is then not in the party's name, in which they claimed to have no interest and cannot provide statements (an older child who refused to provide statements to the Court, asserting this is their information under Art 6 GDPR).

Consider using section 7 of the Banker's Book Evidence Act 1879. You can fill in a D11 application, file a statement and draft order. It is a paper application. It is served on the banks and the respondent. If you have the bank account number and sort code (because you have spotted payments are being made to this account) then you can apply for copies of those account statements directly from the banks, no matter who owns the accounts, as long as the court agrees it is relevant to the case and not a fishing expedition. You pay the costs of the electronic copying and the statements arrive in days of the order being served without the costs of any live hearing. It is a nifty little application. Not one I use very often, but invaluable in the few cases I have needed it. Here is the section 7;

> *"Court or judge may order inspection, etc.*

7. On the application of any party to a legal proceeding a court or judge may order that such party be at liberty to inspect and take copies of any entries in a banker's book for any of the purposes of such proceedings. An order under this section may be made either with or without summoning the bank or any other party, and shall be served on the bank three clear days before the same is to be obeyed, unless the court or judge otherwise directs."

I have always made the application after an order for disclosure has been made against a party and breached, because they say they cannot provide statements for accounts which don't belong to them, or because they have just failed to comply.

Altered Digital Documents

We have to be aware that it is very easy to alter pdfs and screen shots of documents, now. I have come across with colleagues and in my own practice many examples of parties changing figures on a bank statement, or paying small amounts for an internet based company to fill in a blank tax return/ payslip/ bank statement with their own figures: so forging a document.

This is contempt of court, often perverting the course of justice and/or perjury, and there is a recent example of a party being sentenced to 9 months custody for doing this.

You can do 4 things I think to assist with this litigation trick:

(i) listen to your client when they are really sure that a document has been changed;

(ii) check the meta data of a document if you/client have concerns; do this in Adobe (File, Properties, Description and Additional meta data) or Preview (click Tools then Show Inspector) very easily; this tells you who created the document and when and the last time it was amended;

(iii) ask for original documents and not copies or screenshots;

(iv) if you are still concerned issue a Bankers Book Evidence Act 1879 application for the originals from the bank or a Non-Party Disclosure Order against the third party who holds the documents.

Questionnaires

There are no questionnaires of a form E1 provided for under the rules. This means that you cannot raise a questionnaire on the other party's form E1 unless the other side consents to answer it or you have an order of the court permitting you to file and serve one (Rule 19 (4)).

If you do need to raise a questionnaire, and the usual practice is that questions are asked and answered, it is much better if you send it to the other party in advance of the First Appointment. The first hearing can be used to consider if the party takes just exception to any question. You can take instructions on any questions to be added from the client at court. That will save going through that process in correspondence after the hearing which will be more expensive and far more time consuming, or being faced with some smart-alec advocate on the other side pointing out there is no provision under the rules for a questionnaire. Further, if there is any dispute about the proportionality or relevance of a question, the Judge can determine it.

The 2 main reasons to object to a question are that it is irrelevant or disproportionate.

Irrelevant

Many Schedule 1 cases result in overly high legal costs especially when compared to the orders sought. There is no principle of sharing marital acquest in Schedule 1 cases. If the disclosure given shows more than enough capital to meet the claim made by the applicant then there is probably little to be gained from asking detailed questions about the nature or extent of other capital, particularly if it not going to realisable, such as a pension when parties are in their 30s, or later share options. Obviously, the applicant will need to show that the remaining capital will easily provide for the respondent and it may be that demonstrating a small percentage of the respondent's total asset base would be taken up in meeting the applicant's need, is desirable, and a disparity in lifestyle is relevant, but disclosure must be for a purpose.

The applicant's outgoings budget and income available to the applicant, and that includes considering the earning capacity rather than the actual income, is far more relevant in the Schedule 1 case for periodical payments top up, or a lump sum or debts which the applicant says they cannot service, than details of the value of a respondent's shareholding.

Disproportionate

Capital available for meeting the child's need must be set out proportionately. If income is in issue, then it cannot be said that income on a payslip is irrelevant, but if there is a deduction for £2.40 pcm and the income exceeds £1,000 pcm then it is difficult to see how that would be proportionate to seek further disclosure in relation to it.

General Tips on Drafting a Questionnaire

Checklist:

- Always put the correct heading on the document.
- Always ask a question of a paragraph on the Form E/E1, so the first line says "As to Para 1.1" and the second line is the question. You may have more than one question for each paragraph.
- Always go through and check whether the Form E/E1 includes the documents which it requires on the form. Those documents

are set out at the top of the paragraphs in the grey boxes. As a general rule, you should have no issues with proportionality or irrelevance if the document is required by the Form.

- Ask questions which are questions: don't make a statement or a point of analysis: you are giving away your FDR submissions or trial cross examination in advance!

- Don't ask questions which ask if the other party agrees with the following assertion: they may well not and this is an assertion, not a question.

Narrative statement

Do skim read the President's Memorandum on Witness Statements dated November 2021, if you haven't read it for a while.

A narrative statement will need to be filed and served if the matter is going for trial or possibly for a hearing on a preliminary issue or interim provision. You can use the same format as for an ancillary relief section 25 MCA 1973 narrative statements, so background, income, outgoings, needs for capital and income and if possible what you client wants as an outcome, even if within a spectrum of outcomes.

You will also want to work through the criteria for Schedule 1 claims at paragraph 4, as you would the s 25 criteria in financial remedy.

Schedule 1 paragraph 4(1) sets out the checklist which must be considered when assessing a schedule 1 claim and I do not apologise for repeating this a number of times in this text:

'The Court must have regard to *"all the circumstances of the case"* including:

> *(a) the income, earning capacity, property and other financial resources which each person mentioned in sub-paragraph (4) has or is likely to have in the foreseeable future;*
>
> *(b) the financial needs, obligations and responsibilities which each person mentioned in sub-paragraph (4) has or is likely to have in the foreseeable future;*
>
> *(c) the financial needs of the child;*
>
> *(d) the income, earning capacity (if any), property and other financial resources of the child;*
>
> *(e) any physical or mental disability of the child;*
>
> *(f) the manner in which the child was being, or was expected to be, educated or trained.'*

Evidence of needs is the most important, followed by affordability.

A proper budget is needed, and clear evidence of income and income capacity, but also evidence of mortgage capacity and maybe some information on the standard of living if it is very different.

I suppose I draft statements to be read, in a colloquial voice, even if not using colloquial language. The statement is supposed to be in the voice and story of the client. Make sure they agree it and it reflects their views and frankly that they understand it. They will be answering to it in cross examination. I am often met with: "but it wasn't quite like that" and "I didn't write this" … "did you read it?" "yes" "and sign it as true?" "yes" "did you know it was going to be sent to the court for the judge to read?", "yes". You see the point that can be made.

An applicant needs a plan for what order they need the court to make and why. How will it work? What will each party have left in income, liabilities and assets if the court makes the order you seek? This is often called the "net effect" and often the court asks for a schedule of assets as they are before the order and then one after the order sought, to assess this.

I often draft directions to final hearing to attach the draft order sought to a final narrative statement as it helps to concentrate the mind on every little undertaking or recital sought and then nothing is missed. The orders to use are the standard form orders produced for ancillary relief cases. Some, especially the directions orders, have separate paragraphs drafted just for Schedule 1 cases.

The property settlement terms can be complicated: do read them and consider how this might roll over to another property, how is the payer protected, with a fixed sum which increases by CPI, or a percentage share of the property? How does a mortgage affect that if the payee is paying the mortgage?

A respondent needs to show how an applicant can meet their needs on what they are offering. Can they borrow money by way of a mortgage?

Can they work more hours? Will this be a stepped programme of work?

The recent controversial case of *A v B (Schedule 1: Arbitral Award: Appeal) [2024] EWHC 778 (Fam)* saw Cobb J find that it was perfectly appropriate to make an award based upon a payee having to borrow to meet the payments. There has been much chatter about this judgment, but it is not yet appealed as at the time of typing.

CHAPTER TWELVE

PERIODICAL PAYMENTS

Periodical payments are made to the parent or the older child.

Most of the time they will not be relevant unless there are school fees in play or a party has been assessed by the CMS as earning more than £3,000 per week gross after pension contributions.

Where the Court does have jurisdiction, the PPS will be only the CMS amount or cf *James v Seymour [2023] EWHC 833* for the calculations at levels over the cap, and there may be school fees or disability payments in addition (see below).

It bears repeating what I set out earlier (in case you are not reading the book cover to cover). Moor J set out succinctly in *Tony Stacey v Lucy McNicholas [2022] EWHC 278* at paragraphs 27 and 35:

"Section 8(1) of the Child Support Act 1991 applies in any case where a child support officer has jurisdiction to make a maintenance assessment. Section 8(3) states that, in any case where subsection (1) applies, no court shall exercise any power which it would otherwise have to make, vary or revive any maintenance order in relation to the child and absent parent concerned. There are, of course, exceptions, such as where a maximum assessment has been obtained; the child is undertaking education and the order is made solely for the purpose of meeting some or all of the expenses incurred; the child is disabled; or one party resides overseas....

35. I entirely accept that the decision in Dixon v Rennie is correct. The court cannot "top-up" a CMS assessment unless there is a maximum assessment"

A periodical payments order will not therefore be made if the CMS has jurisdiction.

Let us just touch on the big case in this area of *Dickson v Rennie [2014] EWHC 4306 (Fam)* which comes with s 8(6) of the Child Support Act 1991. The parties had not challenged the court's jurisdiction when the Court had made a long term indexed linked periodical payment order in December 2014. F was living out of the jurisdiction. The Judge had assessed his worldwide income and decided it exceeded the maximum cap and so gone on to make an order.

It was in effect a top up order because in the March before that first hearing, F had asked the CMS to make an assessment and it had assessed him on the income he paid himself from his English company, on the basis of his UK tax return, and no worldwide income. The Judge had decided that he had the ability to decide whether the worldwide income was in excess of the CMS assessed UK income and so exceeded the CMS cap, opening the door to a top up order in excess of whatever the CMS recouped.

Under s 8 (1) (3) of the Child Support Act 1991, in any case where the CMS WOULD have jurisdiction, the Court has no jurisdiction. Someone has to have approached them, to have jurisdiction. Under s 8(6) there is an exception to allow top up orders but only when a party's income exceeds the maximum (£3K per week gross after pension contributions).

Holman J decided ONLY the CMS can make that decision. The Court has NO jurisdiction to make that decision, about the extent of a party's income. So even though the DJ found that the F's income was in excess of the maximum cap when taken worldwide, and the CMS cannot look at worldwide income, the DJ had no jurisdiction to make that decision.

F would only pay PPS as assessed by the CMS based upon his paltry UK income which was whatever he decided to pay himself.

Hey-ho.

In *TW v TM (Minors) (Child Maintenance: Jurisdiction and Departure from Formula)* [2016] 2 FLR 1386 Mostyn J stated at paragraph 3 that *Dickson v Rennie* decided that the court has no power to make a *contested* order unless there has been an antecedent maximum assessment. He then stated that by contrast consent orders could be validly made under CSA 1991 s 8(5)(b) by which the court is empowered to make a maintenance order which is in all material respects in the same terms as a prior agreement. That is the extent of the pushing of the *Dickson* boundaries, however: that the parties can agree an order for PPS in excess of the CMS payments.

Back to the general jurisdiction, periodical payments should not normally be made beyond the child's 17th birthday under the Schedule unless the court finds it is right to make the order until the child is 18 years old, usually because they are still in school.

In any event, an order for periodical payments shall not extend beyond a child's 18th birthday (para 3(1)(b) Sch1) unless "*extension conditions*" apply. Those extension conditions are:-

i. the child is, or will be or (if an order were made) would be receiving instruction at an educational establishment or undergoing training for a trade, profession or vocation, whether or not while in gainful employment – para 3(2)(a); or

ii. there are special circumstances which justify the making of an order without complying with that paragraph.

These circumstances of course may include ongoing education or disability including mental health issues. I had a case where the child qualify through neuro-diversity, but the adult child needs to be more than a voluntary NEET (Not in Education, Employment or Training)[29].

29 *Re N (Payments for Benefit of Child) 2009 1 FLR 1442*

The order may take into account the needs of the parent as carer, but this will not exceed what is due under the Child Maintenance Service formula unless there is a top up jurisdiction and/or school fees[30].

School fees may include, as we saw above, lunches, extracurricular activities, or other agreed extras (optional school holidays)

A global budget is a good idea, as per an outgoings schedule.

There is power to vary a PPS order, and to grant interim relief for periodical payments.

An application for interim periodical payments is made under FPR 2010 Part 18, as for financial remedy cf FPR 2010 R 9.7(1)(c) and can even be made before Forms E(1) have been filed as per maintenance pending suit. The rules states that if so, the applicant needs to provide evidence of their needs, financial circumstances and explain why the order is necessary. Under R9.7(4) at least 7 days before the hearing, which should be listed in 14 days from the application, the respondent would have to file and serve their own statement of means.

These applications can be used to in effect secure a Legal Services Payments Order cf below the section on costs

If a payer themself lives from capital there is no reason why they should not pay an order for periodical payments, lump sum or otherwise from that[31].

The case of *A v B (Schedule 1: Arbitral Award: Appeal) [2024] EWHC 778 (Fam),* while criticised in some quarters, is authority for a respondent having to borrow to meet an order.

---

30 *Re P (Child: Financial Provision) 2003 EWCA Civ 837, 2003 2 FLR 865, CA.*

31 *SW v RC 2008 1 FLR 1703*

If the Child Maintenance Service has made an assessment then THAT is your level of periodical payments unless there are grounds for a top up order because they have been assessed by the CMS as over the maximum[32]. The criteria for being over the maximum cap are:

- the payer's income exceeds £3,000 per week gross after pension contributions and so exceeds the maximum for a CMS assessment[33]; or

- there is a need for a school fees order under s 8(7) Child Support Act 1991, which is not a Pps order as such, but a different type of order;

- if the child is disabled or in receipt of Personal Independence Payment, then an order can be made to cover some or all of the expenses incurred due to the child's disability; see below for definitions of disability including "*mental disorder*";[34]

- where the respondent is habitually resident outside the UK, AND the CMS has no jurisdiction to make an assessment the court can make an order, but watch out for those who then pay themselves through an English company to bring themselves within the

---

32 *TW and TM (Minors) 2015 EWHC 3054 (Fam)*

33 *Dickson v Rennie 2014 EWHC 4306 (Fam)*

34 Ss 8(8)(9) Child Support Act 1991. Disability is defined as being blind, deaf, substantially and permanently handicapped by illness, injury, mental disorder, congenital deformity or such other disability as may be prescribed and 'mental disorder' as defined in MHA 1983, s 1(2) as 'mental illness, arrested or incomplete development of mind, psychopathic disorder and any other disorder or disability of mind and 'mentally disordered' shall be construed accordingly". The Equality Act 2010 also defines disability.

CMS jurisdiction;[35]

- adoptive parents are liable to a CMS assessment but not step parents, so a claim against a step parent has to be achieved by way of Schedule 1 or financial remedy claim and they are not caught by the CMS having jurisdiction.

For periodical payments, the question often arises as to how long a periodical payments order should last. The order should not extend beyond the child's 18th birthday and ceasing tertiary education unless the extension conditions apply[36].

I had a case where a disabled adult child was going to need extra time to source a job as they would need significant reasonable adjustments in the workplace and so payments were made for a year after finishing tertiary education but on the basis of special circumstances and the disability.

Example Authority

Length of periodical payments:

Re N (A Child) 2009 EWHC 2096 (Fam), 2010 1 FLR 454, Munby J

The district judge's order deferring sale of a settled property until the child attained 21 years was set aside on appeal; the settlement was varied to end (the property to revert to the payer) when the child attained 18 years and completed tertiary education allowing in addition for one gap year before University.

Many courses are now 4 years long, maybe needing a foundation year and some employers require a Masters. Architecture is renowned for

---

35 S44 Child Support Act 1991

36 Schedule 1 paragraph 3

taking more years than most courses, medicine and vet take 5 years, law has the vocational training element and possibly a conversion year. How far will the Court be persuaded to go in delaying reversion? It will inevitably depend upon how concrete and definite the proposals, how dependent the child in those later years and the resources of the payer. The principle established, however, is until the end of tertiary education after a gap year. The statute allows for it until education ends.

This case was endorsed in the more recent case of *Stacey v McNicholas* *[2022] EWHC 278 (Fam)*.

GW v RW [2003] EWHC 611 (Fam) and Re TW and TM (Minors) [2015] EWHC 3054 (Fam) both per Mostyn J

The payer was a professional footballer player, the court had awarded twice the formula amount as a form of "stockpiling" but it was not a case where a top-up order could be made under s 8(6); father's appeal was therefore allowed and the CMS rate was the limit M could recover.

C v F (Disabled Child: Maintenance Orders) [1998] 2 FLR 1

The child's ongoing disability needs and lack of disclosure led to an extended term beyond the age of 18 years and education.

F v G (Child: Financial Provision) [2004] EWHC 1848 (Fam) Singer J

Father to settle £900K of his £4m assets on mother to house child in London and pay £60,000 of his £500,000 pa income in support.

This was a short relationship which was of course irrelevant, and a 2-year child was cared for by the applicant mother. The father was worth £4m with an annual income of £500,000 pa. The mother had earnings of £37,000 pa but minimal capital.

The father wanted to pay £24K pa to the nanny but to pay it directly himself, school fees at £10K pa and periodical payments of £20K pa (total £54K pa).

Singer J directed the father to settle a lump sum of £900,000 on the purchase of suitable accommodation in Maida Vale, and to make periodical payments of £60,000 pa for the benefit of the child, to include the contribution to nanny costs. All payments were to go to the mother directly for her to control.

This case was reported more than 20 years ago and inflation must be taken into account.

Re N (Payments for Benefit of Child) [2009] 1 FLR 1442

Munby J ordered the mother to give the father receipts for all individual expenditure in excess of £20 for house renovation up to a total of £20,000.

Variation where there has been a periodical payments order

- Either party can apply to vary;
- Variation can encompass suspending or reviving an order[37] which could be a periodical payments order made for the benefit of the child upon divorce or within Schedule 1;
- A variation application can only be brought by a parent if the child is not yet 18 years old and any previous periodical payments order is still live;
- Upon varying a periodical payments order, the Court can make an order for the payment of a lump sum[38];

37 Para 6(2)

38 Para 5(3)

- If the child is aged 16–18 years then the child can apply to revive a dead periodical payments order, as long as one existed before the child was 16 years old (para 6 (5-6);

- If the child is aged over 18 years they could apply for maintenance but only if is there was no order in place immediately before their 16th birthday (para 2(3));

- If the young adult's unmarried parents had settled child maintenance claims to the end of their secondary education, and assuming a subsequent CMS application had not been made to discharge the child maintenance order, the child would be left with nowhere to turn for maintenance in tertiary education;

- The court will not direct lump sum payments in lieu of non-existent or low payments pursuant to the Child Support Act 1991[39]: there is no provision for capitalisation of child maintenance here;

- There is also no jurisdiction for a "clean break" as periodical payments and lump sums can be ordered more than once within the confines of the above rules.

When deciding the application for variation the court shall have regard to all the circumstances of the case, including any change in any of the matters to which the court was required to have regard when making the order[40].

---

39 *Phillips v Peace [1996] 2 FLR 230*

40 Para 6(1)

Section 8 Child Support Act 1991

This section is so important I set out for your reference:

> *"(1) This subsection applies in any case where a child support officer would have jurisdiction to make a maintenance assessment with respect to a qualifying child and an absent parent of his on an application duly made by a person entitled to apply for such an assessment with respect to that child.*
>
> *(2) Subsection (1) applies even though the circumstances of the case are such that a child support officer would not make an assessment if it were applied for.*
>
> *(3) In any case where subsection (1) applies, no court shall exercise any power which it would otherwise have to make, vary or revive any maintenance order in relation to the child and absent parent concerned;*
>
> *(4) Subsection (3) does not prevent a court from revoking a maintenance order;*
>
> ....
>
> *(6) This section shall not prevent a court from exercising any power which it has to make a maintenance order in relation to a child if—*
>
> > *(a) a maintenance assessment is in force with respect to the child;*
> >
> > *(b) the amount of the child support maintenance payable in accordance with the assessment was determined by reference to the alternative formula mentioned in paragraph 4(3) of Schedule 1; and*
> >
> > *(c) the court is satisfied that the circumstances of the case make it appropriate for the absent parent to make or secure the making of periodical payments under a maintenance order in addition to the*

child support maintenance payable by him in accordance with the maintenance assessment.

(7) This section shall not prevent a court from exercising any power which it has to make a maintenance order in relation to a child if—

(a) the child is, will be or (if the order were to be made) would be receiving instruction at an educational establishment or undergoing training for a trade, profession or vocation (whether or not while in gainful employment); and

(b) the order is made solely for the purposes of requiring the person making or securing the making of periodical payments fixed by the order to meet some or all of the expenses incurred in connection with the provision of the instruction or training.

This section shall not prevent a court from exercising any power which it has to make a maintenance order in relation to a child if—

(a) a disability living allowance is paid to or in respect of him; or

(b) no such allowance is paid but he is disabled,

and the order is made solely for the purpose of requiring the person making or securing the making of periodical payments fixed by the order to meet some or all of any expenses attributable to the child's disability.

(9) For the purposes of subsection (8), a child is disabled if he is blind, deaf or dumb or is substantially and permanently handicapped by illness, injury, mental disorder or congenital deformity or such other disability as may be prescribed.

(10) This section shall not prevent a court from exercising any power which it has to make a maintenance order in relation to a child if the order is made against a person with care of the child.

(11) In this Act "maintenance order", in relation to any child, means an order which requires the making or securing of periodical payments to or for the benefit of the child and which is made under—

....

(e) Schedule 1 to the 1989 c. 41. Children Act 1989; .....

and includes any order varying or reviving such an order."

Example Authorities

Re M-M (A child) [2014] EWCA Civ 276

The child had been born in 2003 and had been brought up by mother alone. The father had sought no contact with the child and paid no maintenance. He moved to France. The mother supported herself and the child through state benefits. In 2010 she made contact with the father in France. The mother owned her own home with equity of about £120K. Her claim was for £85K to repair her home and £44K for payment of her significant credit card debts, which she rounded down to £120K. She sought periodical payments of £49K pa. The father worked for an investment company abroad and as a result was outside of the jurisdiction of the Child Maintenance Service (then the CSA). He owned his own property subject to a mortgage, had £137,000 in a bank account and a further £60,000 in a long-term investment. He earned about £70-120K pa including commission and bonus. He had subsequently married and at the time of the hearing had three young children with his wife.

At first instance the order was for:

- £44,620 lump sum to pay debts;

- £1K pcm/£12K pa PPS;

- 15% of Father bonus as PPS.

Both parties appealed. The Court of Appeal heard cross-appeals from the parents in respect of the first instance decision. The periodical payments order had been uncontroversial, but the lump sum award was the focus of the appeal. The Court upheld the order of a lump sum of around one-third of the father's available capital to clear the mother's hard debts:

> *'34. The judge was required to have some regard to the husband's financial resources and the standard of living of his family and the three children who live with him. Equally, his capital resources had a limit to them. In exercising her discretion, and in seeking to achieve an outcome which was fair, just and reasonable, the judge had to balance these factors. She did so by targeting the entirety of her order at the credit card debt with no additional payment of a lump sum directly to the mother. The payment made, however, represented almost exactly a third of the capital that was readily available to the father at the time.'*

The lump sum was not overturned. It represented about 1/3rd of the Father's available capital assets. The periodical payments were about 11.25% of Father's income including £30K pa bonus. That was the relevant CSA percentage for him. Therefore, that psrt of the appeal was dismissed.

As to the bonus, that was reduced from 15% to 11.25% of anything he earned as bonus in excess of £30K because the court was so clear that even periodical payments from the bonus payment had to fall in line with the CSA calculation made at that time.

CHAPTER THIRTEEN

LUMP SUMS

There is no limit to how many lump sums can be ordered: you can go back and bite at that cherry however many times you need to do so.

This section considers the award of lump sums. They are always ordered outright and are not considered repayable, unless they are in effect lump sums to provide housing which is then settled on the payer, to revert at a later date.

In the case of *Tony Stacey v Lucy McNicholas [2022] EWHC 278 (Fam)* Moor J approved HHJ Reardon's order for a lump sum to cover backdated rent, and then a series of lump sums to pay rent pending the payment of the large lump sum for housing. At paragraph 26 he reminded us that: "*Section 5(1) provides that, without prejudice to the generality of paragraph 1, an order under that paragraph for the payment of a lump sum may be made for the purpose of enabling any liabilities or expenses (a) incurred in connection with the birth of the child or in maintaining the child; and (b) reasonably incurred before the making of the order.*"

In *TK v LK [2024] EWFC 71* Nicholas Allen KC at paragraph 77 gave us a useful list:

> *"**Lump sums***
>
> *77. The court has ordered lump sums under Schedule 1 for a wide range of purposes (as a consequence of its expansive interpretation of "for the benefit of the child") including:*
>
> > *a) the furnishing and equipping of a house (Phillips v Peace [1996] 2 FLR 230 and Re P (Child: Financial Provision));*

> *b) the provision of a car (now and every x years) (Re P (Child: Financial Provision) and PG v TW (No. 2) (Child: Financial Provision: Legal Funding) [2014] 1 FLR 508);*
>
> *c) medical, nursing, and hospital costs (Phillips v Peace); and*
>
> *d) payment of the applicant's debts (Morgan v Hill [2007] 1 FLR 1480, Re M-M (Schedule 1 Provision) [2014] 2 FLR 1391, and Re A (A Child: Financial Provision) [2015] 2 FLR 625).*
>
> *78. There is therefore reported authority to support there being jurisdiction for the court to make all of the various lump sums sought by F on Child A's behalf."*

The lump sum award is most often going to be awarded for a clear and specific item of expenditure. There is no entitlement to sharing so the application must identify a need for the lump sum, rather than just "*it would be useful*".

Other common reasons for an award of a lump sum are:

- to pay for debts accrued due to legal costs (although a LSPO should be sought for future costs);
- to renovate an elderly or damp property;
- for a house or rental property deposit; if it is this modest the court may not insist on it being treated as property settlement;
- tuition fees for a Masters or further courses where student loans are not available (unless it is a high net worth case where fee would be paid by parents);
- university accommodation costs
- In the case of a disabled child, there may be costs associated with

equipment, modifications to a house, a new wheelchair, or a one-off respite or holiday.

Nicholas Allen KC continued usefully at paragraph 79:

"Lump sum orders

1. *In Phillips v Peace [2005] 2 FLR 1212 per Singer J the mother argued the court could award a lump sum subject to a condition that it be used towards housing which would in due course revert to the father in accordance with the terms of the original settlement. It was therefore suggested that the lump sum provisions could be used to circumvent the prohibition against ordering a second settlement of property. This was rejected on the basis that it would be a misuse of the court's power. The judge held at [27] that* ***lump sums are not designed to revert to the payer*** *but are paid "once and for all and are used to reimburse past expenditure or are spent on current or future needs. To the extent that whatever was purchased with the lump sum is not consumed it will be retained for or by the child". Lump sum orders therefore do not revert to the paying party."*

So lump sums are never repayable in the way settled property returns to the payer.

A lump sum paying towards past debt

If the court is ordering a lump sum to defray debt, this is a lump sum for monies already expended and so technically is for a retrospective need which has already been met, albeit from borrowing. The court is certainly not averse to an award of a lump sum to cover expenses or debt previously and reasonably incurred already, say in connection with the birth of the child or in maintaining the child or their home. Maybe a party lost their job or their income reduced or they have been sick. I have recently settled a Schedule 1 case at pFDR when the cost of childcare as so high that the high earning single parent with care had run up debt which is to be paid off with a lump sum as part of the order. The other part of the order is for a lump sum to repay the resident parent's mortgage, which sum will be secured as a percentage charge of the house and will revert to the payer when the child finishes education. In the meantime, the mother does not have to pay a mortgage and so has freed up that part of her income for childcare.

In the case of *Morgan v Hill [2007] 1 FLR 1480 (see its own chapter)* there was an award to defray debt incurred through higher housing costs but then it had to be apportioned between 2 children so only 50% of the debt was awarded as a lump sum on appeal.

Example Authority

C v F (Disabled Child: Maintenance Orders) [1998] 2 FLR 1, CA

Payments made to cover costs incurred by a child's disability

Living expenses and school fees are usually met by a periodical payments order, but not always. Where the father's future income was unpredictable as the respondent father was a professional gambler, the court awarded the applicant £254,000 for a school fees fund as future income could be "lumpy". School fees for the youngest child were felt to be too far in the future and so senior school fees for that child were not ordered yet[41]: This is a very unusual order but the facts were also unusual.

Re M-M (A child) [2014] EWCA Civ 276

This case is also set out in the chapter on periodical payments.

The child had been born in 2003 and had been brought up by the mother alone. The father had sought no contact with the child and paid no

41 *Tracey v Tracey [2006] EWCA Civ 734, 2007 1 FLR 196, CA*

maintenance. He moved to France. The mother supported herself and the child through state benefits. In 2010 she made contact with the father in France. The mother owned her own home with equity of about £120K. Her claim was for £85K to repair her home and £44K for payment of her significant credit card debts, which she rounded down to £120K. She sought periodical payments of £49K pa. The father worked for an investment company abroad and as a result was outside of the jurisdiction of the Child Maintenance Service (then the CSA). He owned his own property subject to a mortgage, had £137,000 in a bank account and a further £60,000 in a long-term investment. He earned about £70–120K pa including commission and bonus. He had subsequently married and at the time of the hearing had three young children with his wife.

At first instance in the PRFD the order was for:

- £44,620 lump sum to pay debts;
- £1K pcm / £12K pa PPS;
- 15% of Father bonus as PPS.

Both parties appealed. The Court of Appeal heard cross-appeals from the parents in respect of the first instance decision. The periodical payments order had been uncontroversial but the lump sum award was the focus of the appeal. The Court upheld the order of a lump sum of around one-third of the father's available capital to clear the mother's hard debts:

> *'34. The judge was required to have some regard to the husband's financial resources and the standard of living of his family and the three children who live with him. Equally, his capital resources had a limit to them. In exercising her discretion, and in seeking to achieve an outcome which was fair, just and reasonable, the judge had to balance these factors. She did so by targeting the entirety of her order at the credit card debt with no additional payment of a lump sum directly to*

> *the mother. The payment made, however, represented almost exactly a third of the capital that was readily available to the father at the time.'*

The lump sum was not overturned. It represented about 1/3rd of the Father's available capital assets. The periodical payments were about 11.25% of Father's income including £30K pa bonus. That was the relevant CSA percentage for him. Therefore, that appeal was dismissed.

As to the bonus, that was reduced from 15% to 11.25% of anything he earned as bonus in excess of £30K because the court was so clear that even periodical payments from the bonus payment had to fall in line with the CSA calculation.

CHAPTER FOURTEEN

COSTS

There are four types of orders about costs:

(i) a lump sum to defray a debt which was incurred through legal costs which might even encompass different proceedings;

(ii) a lump sum for future costs in different proceedings which are not LSPO;

(iii) a Legal Services Payment Order;

(iv) costs inter partes, or from the other party, usually due to litigation misconduct.

Let's take them in turn

A lump sum to defray a past costs debt.

This was dealt with in the Lump Sum chapter, so just turn back a few pages to the retrospective lump sum section.

A lump sum for costs in other proceedings

The court has been surprisingly willing to consider this.

Example Authorities

Re S (Child: Financial Provision) [2004] EWCA Civ 1685, 2005 2 FLR 94, CA (Sudan; Sharia law).

Such an order may even establish a 'war chest' for litigation abroad. The child had been taken to Sudan by father and mother needed to apply for the child's return but this was going to be costly and complex as Sharia law was in effect in that part of Sudan, but costs were allowed as an interim lump sum payable by F to M in advance of those proceedings.

R v F (Schedule One: Child Maintenance: Mother's Costs of Contact Proceedings) [2011] 2 FLR 991

An award of a lump sum was made for costs which encompassed legal fees for section 8 child arrangements orders (spend time / live with), and also included costs already incurred.

Legal Services Payment Order

There are many authorities from before LSPOs were available and *Rubin v Rubin* [2014] EWHC 611 (Fam), which confirmed beyond doubt that the jurisdiction to make a LSPO was applicable to Schedule 1.

The earlier authorities, from before *Rubin* in 2014, must be seen in this context and some elements of them may not now be applicable.

Now a lump sum would be used for past costs which are weighing as a debt and a LSPO would be made for future costs, unless there are unusual circumstances where a LSPO would not apply (such as costs for other proceedings). However, some of the older cases do translate as to what is acceptable.

Example Authorities

Here are examples of orders which would now be made by way of LSPO: for future costs by way of lump sum and monthly payments

M-T v T [2006] EWHC 2494 (Fam)

Interim lump sum order for costs

G v G (Child Maintenance: Interim Costs Provision) [2009] EWHC 2080 (Fam)

Costs ordered by way of periodical payments order

The court may award a costs allowance to an applicant who is unable to fund her legal representation, this being seen as 'for the benefit of' the child: Moylan J (although leading counsel brief fee was not allowed and this is maybe the most relevant element of this judgment now).

R v F (Schedule One: Child Maintenance: Mother's Costs of Contact Proceedings) [2011] 2 FLR 991, Bodey J

It is not the court's function to pre-judge the reasonableness of a party's position in the proceedings. Thus, a mother was awarded a costs allowance of £113,000 even where, in related s 8 proceedings, she was opposing contact. Note that in *Rubin,* the strength of the case is a factor to be considered however, and this is a pre-Rubin case.

PG v TW (No 1) (Child: Financial Provision: Legal Funding) [2012] EWHC 1892 (Fam), 2014 1 FLR 508, Theis J

£60,000 was ordered for costs.

A costs allowance should only cover historic unpaid costs where the court is satisfied that, without such a payment, the applicant will not reasonably be able to obtain representation in future.

A party applying for a costs allowance should do so promptly, and the court should approach the matter in a broad way, without being drawn into a detailed examination of the finances and this very much reflects the criteria for LSPOs now.

This is the seminal case on LSPOs

Rubin v Rubin [2014] EWHC 611

Mostyn J gave this judgment about the guidelines for applying for a legal services payments order. He is very clear that these same guidelines should apply to Schedule 1 cases.

"Other orders for legal costs funding

"14. Curiously, the new statutory provisions do not extend to proceedings under Schedule 1 of the Children Act 1989, the Inheritance (Provision for Family and Dependants) Act 1975 or Part III of the Matrimonial and Family Proceedings Act 1984. In such proceedings the application will continue to be for an interim order for this purpose (see, in relation to Schedule 1 proceedings, M-T v T 2007 2 FLR 925, G v G (Child Maintenance: Interim Costs Provision) 2009 EWHC 2080 (Fam), 2010 2 FLR 1264 and CF v KM 2011 1 FLR 208), and the principles in Currey v Currey (No 2) 2006 EWCA Civ 1338, 2007 1 FLR 946 will continue to apply. In that case Wilson LJ stated at para 21 that the applicant must show that he or she cannot reasonably procure legal advice and representation by any other means. Moreover, the subject matter of the application will always be relevant as will be the reasonableness of the applicant's stance in the proceedings.

15. In my opinion the principles set out in para 13 ought to apply, with the necessary modifications, where an order is sought for costs funding in proceedings under Schedule 1 of the Children Act 1989, the Inheritance (Provision for Family and Dependants) Act 1975 or Part III of the Matrimonial and Family Proceedings Act 1984. Obviously, the first sentence of principle (x) will not apply. Whether in these proceedings there is power to make an award for costs funding for ADR is an open question on which I do not venture an opinion here. As regards principle (xii) while there is power under Schedule 1 of the Children Act 1989 and under s5 of the Inheritance (Provision for Family and Dependants) Act 1975 to award a lump sum for costs funding the usual and traditional order is for monthly payments.

Under Part III of the Matrimonial and Family Proceedings Act 1984 monthly payments is the only permissible order. Under each statute there is little scope for a single payment, whether or not deferred in part."

Paragraph 13 of the judgment sets out in fine detail what the procedural and legal guidelines are for whether an application should be granted or not and how to pursue that application. Trying to summarise the para 13 guidance for Schedule 1:

i. Consider s22ZB (1-3) of the Matrimonial Causes Act 1973 which sets out the criteria when seeking a legal services order within financial remedy;

ii. Consider affordability; if a Form E is deficient in disclosure then make robust assumptions against the economically stronger party as to their ability to pay, and do not take what they say at face value;

iii. If a third party has been sustaining a party but appears to have stopped doing so with no reason, the court can assume that the third party's "bounty" will continue, at least until trial;

iv. Be cautious in granting relief for costs if the claim appears tenuous, although there are older authorities which are more robust on this point in favour of the payee;

v. *"The court cannot make an order unless it is satisfied that without the payment the applicant would not reasonably be able to obtain appropriate legal services for the proceedings'*, so only order a payment for past costs if the applicant would not be able to secure future representation without such an order;

vi. It might be reasonable to expect an applicant to charge their home, if they can afford to do so, or if it is likely to be sold at the conclusion of a case, but not to sell it to fund legal costs;

vii. *"Evidence of refusals by two commercial lenders of repute will normally dispose of any issue under s22ZA(4)(a) whether a litigation loan is or is not available;"* try not to use apps with a screenshot with no evidence of the application: the court will want to know what formed the basis of the application, how much was asked for, based upon what income and/or what recovery was anticipated from the litigation etc;

viii. A statement of refusal to enter into a Sears Tooth agreement by the solicitors is usually sufficient to answer this question;

ix. A punitively high-rate loan is usually not reasonable as a means of funding costs and nowadays litigation funders are fairly mainstream although their rates without a guarantor can be 21-24% as standard which is very high and many won't lend for a Schedule 1 claim;

x. *"The order should normally contain an undertaking by the applicant that she will repay to the respondent such part of the amount ordered if, and to the extent that, the court is of the opinion, when considering costs at the conclusion of the proceedings, that she ought to do so. If such an undertaking is refused the court will want to think twice before making the order.";*

xi. Funding will usually only be until FDR and should then be reconsidered;

xii. Funding can be by lump sum (more usual in practice in modest asset cases) or a monthly sum (preferable in higher money cases);

xiii. Make provision in the costs sought for the costs of seeking the LSPO;

xiv. *"A LSPO is designated as an interim order and is to be made under the Part 18 procedure (see FPR rule 9.7(1)(da) and (2)). 14 days' notice must be given (see FPR rule 18.8(b)(i) and PD9A para 12.1).*

The application must be supported by written evidence (see FPR rule 18.8(2) and PD9A para 12.2). That evidence must not only address the matters in s22ZB (1)-(3) but must include a detailed estimate of the costs both incurred and to be incurred. If the application seeks a hearing sooner than 14 days from the date of issue of the application pursuant to FPR rule 18.8(4) then the written evidence in support must explain why it is fair and just that the time should be abridged." Rubin v Rubin [2014] EWHC 611 (Fam) cf paragraph 13 for the criteria and JK v LM [2024] EWHC 1442 (Fam) per Cobb J para 24 et seq for a more recent example of this order in a Schedule 1 case

These are not financial remedy proceedings and so the FPR 2010 R 28 as to costs does not apply to costs awards between parties. Mr Justice Mostyn also says that the usual rule that costs follow the event does not apply either [42].

There are several examples of costs being awarded between parties on appeal but very few on a main application without litigation misconduct.

Do check through the LSPO standard template orders: for example the recipient has to give an undertaking to repay what they do not use.

If responding to such an application look to what other assets could be used for costs but this is not financial remedy, where surrender of a joint cash asset often meets the application.

Look at income and different loan providers.

In a modest asset case consider an interest free credit card or using headroom on an interest only mortgage which is not fully drawn down, selling a second car, or charging a rental property, or even surrendering a small pension under the small pots rules.

---

42 *KS v ND (Schedule 1: Appeal: Costs) 2013 EWHC 464 (Fam), 2013 2 FLR 698*

Could a high monthly payment be shelved during proceedings or trade in the David Lloyd subscription for the local Pure gym?

Could the costs claim be reasonably reduced by instructing direct access counsel, or cheaper solicitors but be aware of optics again if the payer has wealth.

These are claims which will be scrutinsed to the letter so double check the applicant has complied with every part of Rubin and especially the loan applications.

Example Authorities

BC v DE [2016] EWHC 1806 (Fam) Cobb J (15% discount)

The court may set a budget or discount the claim to reflect the usual write-downs on a detailed assessment of costs.

RG v TA (Appeal: Legal Services Funding Order: Schedule 1 Children Act 1989) [2023] EWHC 3155

This is a more recent example of a successful appeal against a refusal to make a legal services payment order to assist with legal funding for child arrangements proceedings and a Schedule 1 application. The mother was from a wealthy family and had received trust monies in the past. She was owed £145,000 by a friend. The father's ability to borrow had been insufficiently considered at first instance. The loan monies were to be divided as a resource to fund litigation costs for both parties by way of a contingent lump sum.

JK v LM [2024] EWHC 1442 (Fam)

Cobb J made a LSPO or costs for a Schedule 1 application, including a preliminary application for a freezing order, and an application in different proceedings for a child arrangements order. F had significant wealth after sale of his interest in an online payment platform to a third party. He had been unforthcoming with disclosure, so a lump sum was also ordered for past costs which were now a debt. He deducted 15% across the board of those figures to reflect notional detailed assessment.

Costs awarded for litigation misconduct

As set out above, Schedule 1 is not subject to FPR 2010 R 28.3 as in financial remedy where the usual order is no order as to costs but in practice few costs orders are made without litigation misconduct or a refusal to engage in NCDR for no good reason.

CHAPTER FIFTEEN

PROPERTY SETTLEMENT AND TRANSFER

Despite the statute setting out in paragraph 1(2) (e) of Schedule 1 that property may be transferred to a parent or a child, there remain no significant reported cases on this save for a Russian oligarch (overturned on appeal) and an exceptional case of a parent imprisoned for traumatising a child who was left with significant long-term needs[43].

The Court of Appeal considered the circumstances in which *outright* capital provision could or should be made for a child, in the oligarch case, one of whom had already turned 18 years. It concluded that special circumstances required to be shown for outright provision, and that those circumstances had to relate to the child in question and to a consequent continuing financial need into adulthood.

The court allowed F's appeal against an order that he provide funds outright for the purchase of homes for two children once they reached adulthood, made on the basis that he might otherwise use his financial muscle to impose some form of 'financial ultimatum' on them.

The almost invariable practice is for property to be settled for the minority of the child, even if the payer is fabulously wealthy and for it then to revert back to the payer.

---

43 UD v DN (Schedule 1, *Children Act 1989*; Capital Provision) *[2021] EWCA Civ 1947* is the oligarch and TK v LK [2024] EWFC 71 is the imprisoned parent

You can only have one property order. You can however have an order for rental payments pending the purchase of that order and that has been done by a series of lump sums.

The Court will not allow a subsequent lump sum order for further housing by the back door[44].

It could allow payments to improve, maintain or repair a property[45].

Example Authorities

Mr Justice Ward J noted in *A v A (A Minor: Financial Provision) [1994] 1 FLR 657* that "*exceptional circumstances*" would be needed before such an order could be made and ***"property adjustment orders should not ordinarily be made to provide benefits for the child after he has attained his independence."*** *(p661)*

MT v OT (Financial Provision: Costs) [2007] EWHC 838 (Fam), 2008 2 FLR 1311, Charles J, noted that the child's minority is usually held to be until the end of tertiary education which is 1st degree and gap year[46].

However, if the parties have lived together, if a property was held in joint names, or there is evidence it was intended to be owned by both parties, you may have a trusts of land application to establish a beneficial interest which could be heard alongside Schedule 1 and this could lead to a transfer of property / beneficial interest outright. The court may also

44 Phillips v Peace [2005] 2 FLR 1212

45 H v C [2009] EWHC 1527

46 *Re N (Payments for Benefit of Child) 2009 EWHC 11 (Fam), 2009 1 FLR 1442, Munby J.*

regulate the occupation of a property this way[47] or make orders about how a property should be occupied using this same legislation.

The applicant's housing needs after the child has no need for the home, are not relevant. There is no need to debate how they will house themselves when the settled property reverts to the payer as their needs are not in issue.

Further, if the applicant cohabits, then that might affect their needs for income, if they have someone else contributing but that cohabitee has no duty to house the child, so to that end the cohabitation is irrelevant to housing need[48].

The settlement should not come with conditions, such as not moving abroad[49]. It may allow, and often does, rolling over the equity into another property. For the details of how this works, look to the standard template orders.

A transfer or settlement of property order may be made either to the child themselves (although this would be unusual) or to the applicant for the benefit of the child.

It is possible under these provisions to direct the transfer of a council tenancy from one parent to the other, although the power should obviously be sparingly exercised.[50]

---

47 *Pearson v Franklin 1994 1 WLR 370, CA*

48 *F v G (Child: Financial Provision) [2004] EWHC 1848*

49 *G v S(Children Act 1989: Schedule 1) [2017] EWHC 365 (Fam), Hayden J.*

50 Para 1(2)(e).

Example Authorities

F v G (Child: Financial Provision) [2004] EWHC 1848 (Fam), 2005 1 FLR 261, Singer J

You have seen this case in a previous chapter.

Father to settle £900K of his £4m assets on mother to house child in London and pay £60,000 of his £500,000 pa income to her by way of child support.

This was a short relationship which was of course irrelevant, and a 2-year child was cared for by the applicant mother. The father was worth £4m with an annual income of £500,000 pa. The mother had earnings of £37,000 pa but minimal capital.

The father wanted to pay £24K pa to the nanny but to pay it directly himself, school fees at £10Kpa and periodical payments of £20K pa (total £54K pa).

Singer J directed the father to settle a lump sum of £900,000 on the purchase of suitable accommodation in Maida Vale, and to make periodical payments of £60,000 pa for the benefit of the child, to include the contribution to nanny costs. All payments were to go to the mother directly for her to control.

This case was reported 14 years ago and inflation must be taken into account.

DE v AB [2011] EWHC 3792 (Fam)

A modest asset case. Respondent earned £100K pa but applicant in receipt of benefits with large debts (£170k) and modest house equity (£98K), albeit she was accruing debt paying for the mortgage. Payer ordered to settle 81% of his assets, £250,000 of his £358,000 own house equity on her to house her without a mortgage. In addition, he had to pay her £40K outright lump sum to assist in defraying her debts. The £250K would return to him, the £40K was an outright lump sum.

At first instance before the District Judge, the mother was earning £60K pa and additional commission but by the time of the appeal she was receiving job seekers allowance. Her home had equity of £98K. She had liabilities of £111,385 which were £170K by the time of the hearing. The father had been a city trader but had been made redundant in 2004, so some years before, but on a redundancy package of £952,000. He had enjoyed it and now had only the £358,000 equity in his house and no other assets. He earned about £100K pa. On appeal, Baron J, sitting in the High Court, upheld the first instance award of £250,000 for settled housing as *'completely unappealable'*

However, she reduced the lump sum awarded to be paid towards the Mother's debts to £40,000. Thus, the father paid £290,000 (81% of his assets), to the Mother albeit only about 11% was transferred outright. He then had enough left for a house deposit.

TK v LK [2024] EWFC 71

I have referenced this judgment several times in this book already and at the top of this chapter. It is very useful and digestible. There was one child. That child had lived with mother but after she committed a serious crime against the child, they moved to live with father. Father and child were living outside of the jurisdiction to preserve their own safety. Mother was serving a long prison sentence for the crime. She appeared convinced, and had an army of internet supporters behind her, that the child had been the subject of satanic and ritualistic abuse from father since birth. There was no plausible evidence of this.

There had been financial remedy proceedings between the parties and a full capital and income clean break order which long predated the Schedule 1 proceedings. However, the court found that these facts were exceptional (the test for an order after a full clean break). The court was therefore willing to make further lump sum orders.

M had inherited from her father, although her disclosure about it was patchy and she was not clear that she had any realizable sums from it.

The Court drew adverse inferences against her, given her lack of credibility and poor disclosure record, and found that she had £341K at her disposal from that inheritance.

The behaviour of M had been so egregious and its effects so significant it would be inequitable to disregard it.

The assessment of whether there are 'special' or 'exceptional' circumstances must focus on the child's dependency, said the Judge, rather than their vulnerability, as not everyone with a vulnerability is 'dependent' in the sense of requiring financial support; see paragraphs 79–89 and he quoted *UD v DN supra.* In other words, this is about needs.

The Judge confirmed that *Re P (Child: Financial Provision)* [2003] EWCA Civ 837 remained the seminal authority for Schedule 1 cases and noted that HHJ Hess in *SP v QR* [2024] EWFC 57 highlighted again that Schedule 1 cases were not limited to the '*affluent to fabulously rich*' but could be just as applicable to modest asset cases.

The Judge found that:

(i) F could probably no longer secure a mortgage and his earning capacity was negatively affected by M's conduct;

(ii) M continued to pose a threat to the child who had PTSD and trauma as a result of her actions; F had only left her alone for 90 minutes and she had been calling him in tears, asking him to go home and so she had a higher need for stability and a mortgage free house without the risk of repossession;

(iii) M continued to state that the child had been subjected to satanic abuse since the day they were born by F and her supporters online were ranged to support her cause and posed an ongoing threat to the child on her behalf;

(iv) The child had a housing need for a 2 -3 bedroomed modest property at £384K. The child should not have to use their £32.7K savings towards this. F had £100K by way of inheritance which should be used;

(v) £10,000 was ordered by way of further lump sum to meet child's therapeutic needs;

(vi) £15,500 by way of further lump sum was ordered for a car for F to drive child around;

(vii) The order was therefore for £309,750 outright lump sum, none of which should revert on a settlement basis to M, but all was paid on a lump sum outright basis.

This case had exceptional facts but it is very readable and useful in explaining the legal thought processes and application of those in a modest asset case.

MT v OT [2018] EWHC 868 Cohen J made provision for the purchase of a replacement property in a different area and found this was not a second settlement: he was ordering a lump sum for the costs of the relocation, not a further lump sum for property settlement. This case is examined further in the next chapter.

CHAPTER SIXTEEN

SUBSEQUENT ORDERS

The Court can revisit periodical payments, lump sums and secured provision but not make more than one property settlement or transfer orde[51]. If there has been housing provision by way of lump sum, then it has to be said the Court is not going to order another housing lump sum, for a different property because technically lump sums can be made endless times. It would look at further lump sums for works, repairs, maintenance of the property and/or debts and maybe even for moving and rolling a settlement over into another property, but not for more property or a better property.

Orders in Subsequent Applications.

Children can be dependent for a long time and circumstances can change. What can the court do if an order needs to be revisited or a new claim made for a category of order that was not sought the first time around?

- If the **child is aged between 16–18 years** then the child can apply to vary, or even to revive an order which has ceased to have effect as long as the child does so before their 18th birthday[52];

- There can be **more than one (secured) periodical payments order or lump sum order made before the child attains the age of 18 years**, for the same payee to or for the benefit of the same child;

[51] *Para 1(5)(b)*

[52] Schedule 1 para 6(5 - 6).

- There can be **variation, discharge, suspension or revival** of a secured or unsecured periodical payments order or lump sum order;

- Paragraph 10 gives the remit when seeking a **variation of a maintenance agreement**; see ***Morgan v Hill*** under the chapter "Blended Families" for an example of this;

- The court **cannot make more than one settlement or transfer of property** order against the same party in respect of the same child;

- However, the statute provides the power to vary, suspend, rescind or revoke a final order:

"25. Section 31F (6) of the Matrimonial and Family Proceedings Act 1984 provides that the Family Court has power to vary, suspend, rescind or revive any order made by it. This provision is given procedural effect by Family Procedure Rules 2010 Part 4.1(6) which provides that the Family Court may vary or revoke an order."

Example Authority

Re C (A child) Schedule 1 Children Act Variation [2018] EWFC B40,

There had been a final schedule 1 order made in 2014 in this jurisdiction. Pursuant to that Order, the father was paying periodical payments of £4,500 pcm to the mother and he provided £700,000 for housing her and the child. Father and child now lived together in Canada, and the mother remained in England. The fact that the mother was living in this jurisdiction and that this was a variation application of an existing order made in that same jurisdiction, gave the court power to act. The Child Support Act 1991 did not apply as to periodical payments because the father was living out of the jurisdiction.

HHJ Booth gave a learned judgment and noted that, as set out above, the court had power to revoke or vary a previous order, even for settlement of property. He said that usually the court would need one of the following grounds to be met for the order to be varied, suspended, rescinded or revived:

> *(a) where there has been a material change of circumstances since the order was made; or*
>
> *(b) where the facts on which the original decision was made were (innocently or otherwise) misstated*[53].

These are useful guidance. The change of circumstances in this case had been that the child had lived with the mother and now lived with the father. The periodical payments order was discharged, and the lump sum for settled property provision was varied from £700,000 to £200,000 to allow the mother enough to house herself in a modest 2 bedroomed flat or small house, in the UK and that would be for the benefit of the child when he visited her. The property would revert to the father when the child had finished secondary and tertiary education and attained 18 years old. The father was wealthy, with a good income, but this sum met the needs of the situation. The child was only going to spend 8 weeks a year in England with his mother (and she would see him further in Canada). The father had been ordered in the child arrangement proceedings (which had been up as far as the Court of Appeal), to pay towards the travel costs for the child arrangements.

Phillips v Peace [2004] EWHC 3180 (Fam) Singer J

There was no power to award a further lump sum for the purpose of providing larger accommodation years after the event.

53 *CS v ACS 2015 EWHC 1005 (Fam)*

H v C [2009] EWHC 1527 (Fam) HHJ Judge Barnett QC sitting as Dep High Court judge:

The mother was not bound by a prior agreement to accept a certain property settlement and not to claim a future lump sum, in circumstances where the respondent father had been guilty of non-disclosure. See also the case of *Morgan v Hill* above where the mother was also not held to a prior agreement which did not meet the child's needs.

MB v KB [2007] EWHC 789 (Fam)

When divorce and financial remedy took place there were no assets available; when father came into money some years later mother was allowed to apply for a property settlement award under Schedule 1 where none had been made on the first application

The parties had been married and the applicant had not sought property in the financial remedy proceedings as her and the child's housing needs had been met by a rented property; the respondent had had no resources at that time; later the respondent came into money and the applicant applied this time under Schedule 1 for housing; the respondent tried to have the application struck out for issue estoppel but Baron J found that the child's needs and circumstances had changed, and she was allowed to bring the claim.

PK v BC (Financial Remedies: Schedule 1) [2012] EWHC 1382 (Fam)

Applicant brought Schedule 1 proceedings after financial remedy proceedings had awarded her a lump sum for housing. She had no further need, ad no exceptional circumstances so no order made.

A persistent applicant sought housing provision under Schedule 1 after she had been awarded £950,000 for housing in previous financial remedy proceedings; the respondent's position had deteriorated in the meantime, but the applicant nevertheless came back for more money for housing under Schedule1. Moor J accepted the proceedings were valid but, on these facts, refused any award to the applicant because the child's needs were met.

MT v OT [2018] EWFC 868 (Fam)

Was Mother resettling in a different property, in fact rolling over the capital, or seeking a second property settlement order?

What size of fund should the father provide for tertiary education?

There were also issues as to security of payment with a father who lived largely out of the jurisdiction.

Factual background:

The children were twins born on 20th June 2001 and so they were at the point of the hearing 17 years old. There were three extant applications by the applicant mother carer and one by the respondent father. Both parents had been found by a Judge to be dishonest witnesses: the court found that the mother would exaggerate her claims and that the father would make promises he did not keep. The parties had been locked in various forms of litigation about the children since about 2005. The relationship was acrimonious and the parents did not trust each other. There had been a contact / child arrangements order but the father had not seen the children since 2005.

There had been various enforcement proceedings about the payment of money judgments. Due to the father's failure to pay in the past, all parties had agreed at a previous hearing that the father would pay a lump sum (to include index linking) to the mother's solicitors and those solicitors would administer the money and pay monthly sums from it, to her. That is what was happening by the time of this hearing.

Rehousing:

- Father ran a quasi-millionaire's defence. He said he was worth at least £40m and earned at least £780K pa. Mother lived in North London at the top of the Great North Way (A1). The Mother sought a new property. She did not like the one they were in as there had been a lot of building and she had not been able to maintain it to a good standard. She wished to trade up. Father said it was more than adequate and to trade up would be a second property settlement which is not permitted under Schedule 1.

- The Judge found:

  "19..... The replacement of one property by another does not amount to a new settlement of property. It is simply the substitution of one property for another......."

  22. I recognize that the father will "lose" in the region of £100,000 by way of the irrecoverable costs of sale and purchase. I do not overlook that, but I need to see it in the context also of his overall wealth and the needs of the children.

  23. In my judgment it is reasonable for the mother and girls to require to be housed elsewhere. I direct that the mother shall be permitted to choose a replacement property for herself and the children which shall be purchased for their occupation on the same terms as before subject to the power of the father to veto the property if it is not a proper investment of his funds.

  24. The question then arises as to the value of the housing fund. The property has been valued by the SJE at £1.35 million. The value reflects the condition of the property. If it had been maintained and updated in the way that it might have been by the father, then it would have been worth more.

25. The mother accepts that the costs of sale and the legal costs and SDLT of the new purchase should come out of the proceeds of sale. However, she asks that she should be provided with the sum of £2,500 towards removals and £47,500 for what she describes as "kitting out". Thus, she seeks from the father, the sum of £1.4 million.

26. I direct and order as follows:

i) The father may, if he so wishes, keep the property for himself and provide the mother with £1.35 million plus the further sums that I set out below.

ii) If the property is sold, the father shall provide the mother with a housing fund, out of which the costs of sale and purchase shall be paid, in a sum which is the greater of £1.35 million or the actual sum obtained upon sale. It is the mother who will have to bring up the children in the new house and, bearing in mind the extent of the father's wealth, it would not be appropriate that the mother and children should bear the consequences of any sale at less than £1.35 million.

iii) The father shall pay the additional sum of a maximum of £50,000 of which not more than £25,000 may be spent by the mother on equipping the property and removals and the balance of which may be spent on works to the property. The sum spent on works will in due course accrue at least to some extent for the father's benefit as the property will eventually revert to him. The sum spent on equipping the property and removals is a necessary incidence of moving from a property bought some 10/11 years ago and when the children were very much younger.

iv) The mother will be entitled to take with her to the new property the furniture in the current home."

Periodical payments

- The children were at different boarding schools. Mother visited each child once a week and this took up most of the day. She then had them home in holidays (22 weeks a year at least) and for the odd weekend. "*It is plain that the girls miss one another and, in their different ways, each is struggling.*"The children had identified learning needs.

- Mother had been a lawyer in Nigeria before the children were born and Father said she could work and earn a living. She had done little paid work for 20 years. The somewhat surprising finding in 2018 from Mr Justice Cohen was that she had no earning capacity at all.

- Term:

  The Judge considered 7 total years of payments should be funded after school on the basis one child may take a 3-year degree and the other a 4-year degree. There was no provision for a gap year.

The Judge ordered Father to pay:

- £7,500 pcm for both children whilst the girls remained at school and £6,500 pcm whilst they were at University or on a gap year for 7 years (3.5 years each). Of the latter, £3K pcm was for the girls (£1.5K each) and £3.5K pcm for the mother as carer;

- There were then university accommodation costs and student fees on top: 7 years of tuition fees were ordered, 7 years of £12K pa = £84K for accommodation and £5K per child for kitting out for tertiary education years = £94K;

- The Judge made an order for extra tuition fees based upon an expert's report and the children's identified study needs;

- There was an order for £5K pa for dental and medical care for both children;
- There were then sums for mother's debts, legal fees and a car.

At paragraph 46 the Judge set out the award. It was all to be paid to the mother, including the fees for University and accommodation costs but then the father and children had had no contact since 2005 and there was a history of poor payment. Note the fees for solicitors to administer the fund.

Capital Sums: (Para 14)	£43,612 + interest
Extra Housing costs (Para 26)	£50,000
School Fees and Extras: (Para 32)	£121,900
Insurance/Property M'ntce. (Para 33)	£27,500
Periodical payments: (Para 36/37)	£447,000
Tertiary education (Para 40)	£158,750
Extra Tuition Costs: (Para 42)	£32,880
Other Professional Costs (Para 44)	£27,500
Administration Costs (Para 45)	£7,920
Total:	£917,062 + interest

CHAPTER SEVENTEEN

TRUSTS OF LAND CLAIMS

These claims are so common in conjunction with Schedule 1 that they deserve to be the last chapter. You will need to consult more worthy texts for a full exposition of this area of law, but here are some very basic tips and indicators. You sometimes need TLATA for an interim order for sale or declaration as to right to occupy.

The separate civil proceedings are listed alongside your Schedule 1 proceedings but they are subject to the CPR. In NCDR you can of course ask your pFDR judge or arbitrator or mediator to consider all of the issues together. I have been at many court based FDRs where the Judge will consider all issues together but getting to that point can be costly, as the separate proceedings need different preparation.

If you issue trusts of land proceedings then the Court can enforce that. The court does not have the power under Schedule 1 to make a TLATA order for declarations of beneficial interest, however, so if you do not issue, then the Court will not be considering beneficial interests or the criteria for those.

This can be a tricky choice between a costly disproportionate route and ruling out some of the Court's powers, and limiting the law it is applying, when you are not quite sure of the other side's case. Maybe this is a good reason to get everyone into NCDR and you can scope out what is being said on the other side.

A trusts of land claim might give your client a right to a share in the equity, the ownership of a property which has been a joint home of unmarried cohabitants whereas a Schedule 1 claim will only give rise to a possible claim for periodical payments, and a lump sum and settlement of property, rather than an interest in the property.

If the property is held in joint names, that is likely to be your answer, as to ownership and division of the equity when it is sold, unless you have other documentation such as other trust deeds. You will the possibly need only Schedule 1 to delay sale, a property settlement order to allow the child to live in the payer's share of the property until they finish school. If the property is held in the name of one party, and your applicant client believes it was agreed that they have an interest in the property, and/or they have paid significant sums towards its purchase or renovation, then TLATA proceedings or s 37 MPPA 1970 proceedings are far more likely.

TLATA can be used to stop a property being sold and to determine final occupation rights. Schedule 1 is only really used for the delay of sale and occupation right until the child finishes school or University.

The first thing to establish in a trusts of land claim is whether there is joint or single ownership of the property.

If there is joint legal ownership, the presumption is that the beneficial ownership is the same as the legal ownership.

If your client's name is not on the deeds / at the Land Registry as a joint owner, then you are trying to establish a claim. That is a two-step process: do they have a share and then what size of share?

How to explain equity to a client? Back in the days of Magna Carta at Runnymede, in the 13th century, the types of case which could come before the Courts were very heavily circumscribed. Magna Carta introduced a system to allow the petitioning of the King for relief in a meritorious case which fell outside of these strict rules. This was confirmed by a statute of Parliament in 1406. This is the same authority which was used to gave rise to the 6 million Second Referendum (Brexit) petitions and the e-petitions of today. Eventually, the king became overwhelmed/bored and gave responsibility for these petitions to the king's counsellor, later called the Chancellor. In time, this system became a court, the court of Chancery, the scene of the odd Gilbert and Sullivan Victorian operetta, and Dickens' *Jarndyce v Jarndyce* and the subject of many satirical cartoons. It has grown up as a parallel system to the courts of Kings Bench and Common Pleas, and has become the system of equity which sits alongside and often overrides the legal certainties of the other courts, in order to make everything right, like the deep magic of Narnia. It is not a court of fairness, like a daytime television show where the audience calls out its judgment upon contestants or "guests". It has rules, statute and precedent, like any other area of law.

The Law Commission has brought forward a consultation paper and proposals for legislation to assist co-habitants to clarify this law for them, and make it more accessible, its exercise more certain, but none has made it onto the statute books. Scotland has managed it with the Scotland under Family Law (Scotland) Act 2006 and Australia has a very similar system. England and Wales does not.

9 out of 10 couples will now cohabit in some form at some point in their relationship, without being married. There is still no clear understanding about the cohabitant's legal position amongst the general public where myths such as "common law spouse" still stubbornly persist at a terrifyingly high level.

In *Burns v Burns [1984] Ch 317* a woman lived with a man and brought up his children for 20 years, changed her name and made her home in the family home. She was, however, entitled to no beneficial interest in the family property, nor maintenance and the law has not changed such that any different result would be achieved today.

Here, I have concentrated on the principles of whether your client may or may not have a claim, rather than the details of a civil TLATA claim as you are likely to run that alongside your Schedule 1 claim.

What is a trusts of land claim?

It is usually a dispute over interests in property, either the money value of the bricks and mortar or an endowment policy or it can regulate a right to live in a property. It can involve a third party who may have put money into the property, a promise that a person is to have an interest now or upon certain conditions or in the future or an agreement that they are to have such an interest.

Acquiring a beneficial interest involves transferring an interest in property to someone who does not have it beforehand. The system would fall apart if transfers of interests in property could be made by drunken late night rambling text messages, chance remarks or a row in the car. They involve an agreement intentionally made between 2 people and evidenced by their words, or actions.

The area of law is called TLATA or TOLATA after the Trusts of Land and Appointment of Trustees Act 1996. Sections 12–15 Trusts of Land and Appointment of Trustees Act 1996 are the central ones which include all that you really need. These sections are always the place to start. Section 12 sets out how a beneficial interest gives a right to occupy a property and s13 sets out how a court may restrict that right

> *"14. Applications for order.*
>
> *(1) Any person who is a trustee of land or has an interest in property subject to a trust of land may make an application to the court for an order under this section.*
>
> *(2) On an application for an order under this section the court may make any such order—*
>
> > *(a) relating to the exercise by the trustees of any of their functions (including an order relieving them of any obligation to obtain the consent of, or to consult, any person in connection with the exercise of any of their functions), or*
> >
> > *(b) declaring the nature or extent of a person's interest in property subject to the trust, as the court thinks fit.*

(3) The court may not under this section make any order as to the appointment or removal of trustees.

(4) The powers conferred on the court by this section are exercisable on an application whether it is made before or after the commencement of this Act."

15. Matters relevant in determining applications.

(1) The matters to which the court is to have regard in determining an application for an order under section 14 include—

(a) the intentions of the person or persons (if any) who created the trust,

(b) the purposes for which the property subject to the trust is held,

(c) the welfare of any minor who occupies or might reasonably be expected to occupy any land subject to the trust as his home, and

(d) the interests of any secured creditor of any beneficiary.

(2) In the case of an application relating to the exercise in relation to any land of the powers conferred on the trustees by section 13, the matters to which the court is to have regard also include the circumstances and wishes of each of the beneficiaries who is (or apart from any previous exercise by the trustees of those powers would be) entitled to occupy the land under section 12.

(3) In the case of any other application, other than one relating to the exercise of the power mentioned in section 6(2), the matters to which the court is to have regard also include the circumstances and wishes of any beneficiaries of full age and entitled to an interest in possession in property subject to the trust or (in case of dispute) of the majority (according to the value of their combined interests).

(4) This section does not apply to an application if section 335A of the Insolvency Act 1986 (which is inserted by Schedule 3 and relates to applications by a trustee of a bankrupt) applies to it.

Then section 15 is the matters to be considered under the statute

"15. Matters relevant in determining applications.

(1) The matters to which the court is to have regard in determining an application for an order under section 14 include—

(a) the intentions of the person or persons (if any) who created the trust,

(b) the purposes for which the property subject to the trust is held,

(c) the welfare of any minor who occupies or might reasonably be expected to occupy any land subject to the trust as his home, and

(d) the interests of any secured creditor of any beneficiary.

(2) In the case of an application relating to the exercise in relation to any land of the powers conferred on the trustees by section 13, the matters to which the court is to have regard also include the circumstances and wishes of each of the beneficiaries who is (or apart from any previous exercise by the trustees of those powers would be) entitled to occupy the land under section 12.

(3) In the case of any other application, other than one relating to the exercise of the power mentioned in section 6(2), the matters to which the court is to have regard also include the circumstances and wishes of any beneficiaries of full age and entitled to an interest in possession in property subject to the trust or (in case of dispute) of the majority (according to the value of their combined interests)."

The proceedings rules

The Civil Procedure Rules will always apply unless the case is consolidated or run with a family case such as a Schedule 1 Children Act 1989 case, when the FPR 2010 will probably be applied by the Court.

Under the CPR, a trusts of land claim should be issued under part 7 or 8 as follows:

<u>Issue</u>

Part 7: A claim form N1 and read the guidance at N1A and Particulars of Claim, followed by Defence. This is used when there is a dispute of fact as to the dealings between the parties and their intentions.

Part 8: A claim form and statement of fact in support. No pleadings are needed. This is like the old originating summons procedure and is used when there is no real dispute of fact, for example when you just need a property sold or you know the ownership and shares but need to just get the money out.

Case management and disclosure then follows and the matter is referred to the District Judge for directions. The District Judge may or may not make directions as to costs rules including costs budgets in Part 8 claims but the rules as to costs budgets are mandatory for Part 7. In these cases, it is highly likely the court will make no order as to costs budgets if the claim is under Part 8. It is likely they will list the case alongside the Schedule 1 claim and will follow the FPR thereafter, asking any third parties to set out their case so it can be examined at FDR.

The fact that Part 8 has no mandatory rules on costs budgets is often a reason to issue under Part 8 rather than Part 7 if there is the option to choose, and a witness statement can be easier to draft than a pleading.

All of this means you should be ready to fill in a costs budget form, 1 page or the full thing, when you get your first directions form if you are issuing parallel proceedings but within Schedule 1 proceedings you may well have the proceedings joined, or the issue subsumed into the Schedule 1, and the FPR applied by the Court.

Trusts

Remember the issues will be:

i. Is it sole or joint ownership;

ii. What is there in writing from the time? Look for attendance notes from the solicitor's conveyancing file and secure the file in full. Contemporaneous e-mails, or those written before everyone falls out can help to show intention and may even be sufficient to transfer legal ownership under s2 Law of Property Miscellaneous Provisions Act 1989 or beneficial ownership under 53 (1)(c) of the Law of Property Act 1925[54];

iii. If the property is jointly owner, then what are the shares? Did they even think about it? If not, what do their actions suggest? If nothing, what is fair?

iv. Is there any equitable accounting to take place after the shares have been determined? That is any adjustment to allow for the fact that since separation only one of 2 owners has paid the mortgage? Or one has paid for maintenance or upkeep. Has one party been excluded from the property, in which case they might be able to claim an occupation rent from the person living in their share of the property.

---

54 Hudson v Hathway [2022] EWCA 1648 (Civ) :

v. Is there a right to occupy under certain terms or for a certain time?

A party can generate an interest in a property usually by a constructive trust, proprietary estoppel or s37 of the MPPA 1970. Resulting trusts are rarely used now.

The relevant and up to date case law is all focussed on intention, rather than contributions: cf *Marr v Collie [2017] UKPC 17*.

The right to live under certain terms, say a Granny who has given money for an annexe in exchange for a right to stay there rent free for life, is almost always generated by constructive trust or proprietary estoppel.

Is there an express declaration of trust?

Is there an express, written or spoken, declaration of trust? If so, this will likely be determinative of the matter it sets out, and whether it is intended that a non-legal owner had an interest or what the shares of a joint ownership might be, or what the terms of occupation might be.

Evidence Checklist

- Check the paperwork; this means any written declaration, dated and signed as to beneficial interests in the property;
- Look at the TR1 (for a transfer post 1.4.1998), the conveyance document, as this can also include such a declaration;
- Look at the HMLand Registry to see if there is any express declaration of trust held there and ask the client if there was a trust deed;

- Look at the conveyancing files; ALWAYS seek disclosure of them if they still exist; if the solicitors had joint clients then your client is entitled to a copy, even if not the original file.

If there is an express declaration of trust it is likely that will be an end to the matter[55]. Setting aside an express declaration can only be done in one of the following circumstances:

- Fraud;
- Sham;
- Proprietary estoppel;
- Undue influence;
- Non est factum;
- New agreement;

There is a significant legal debate as to whether a fresh agreement which changes the shares can be oral when the original express declaration was in writing, or even just in writing where the original agreement was a deed. The most recent case[56] suggests this is possible, but many other judgments say it is not.

---

55 *Goodman v Gallant 1986 1 FLR 53* and post TR1 the case is *Pankhania v Chandegra 2012 EWCA Civ 1438*

56 *Re Cynberg* [2024] EWHC 2164 (Ch) and see the very helpful discussion on the point at https://financialremediesjournal.com/content/they-think-it-s-all-over-it-is-not-express-declarations-subsequent-agreements-and-the-decision-in-em-re-cynberg-em.348e305cd116414c962db3d15161fc33.htm

Old Fashioned conveyance. The recording in a conveyance that the survivor of two joint beneficial owners can give valid receipt on a disposition, does not, in itself, prove to be a declaration of beneficial joint ownership. However, if the parties understood it to mean the right to survivorship would apply then the evidence of beneficial joint tenancy intention is strong.

What are resulting and constructive trusts or the ways that a beneficial interest may be found?

Resulting Trusts

Lord Neuberger rejuvenated these 20 years ago in Stack v Dowden. By and large they refer to a share based upon actual contribution to purchase unless there is an agreement otherwise. That can include mortgage payments and funding extensions. They tend to be used to analyse investment properties and properties bought even in family arrangements but not cohabiting couples. Lord Neuberger gave a dissenting judgment in the seminal case of *Stack v Dowden [2007] 2 AC 432*. He wanted to analyse the shares of a property bought by a cohabiting couple by way of resulting trust as what they had paid was the only clear evidence, as he saw it, of intention. He was outvoted. and constructive trusts now are used for cohabiting couples and resulting trusts are falling away even for family investment properties.

Again in *Jones v Kernott [2012] 1 AC 776*, the Supreme Court stated: *"the time has come to make it clear...that in the case of the purchase of a house or flat in joint names for joint occupation by a married or unmarried couple, where both are responsible for any mortgage, there is no presumption of a resulting trust arising from their having contributed to the deposit (or indeed the rest of the purchase) in unequal shares"*

The name for them probably comes from the Latin resalire which means to jump back: so the property held by the legal owner, or part of the property, jumps back or "results" back to the person who paid for it.

Interesting, but probably not very relevant for your parties who have a child.

Constructive Trusts

These are based upon the parties' agreements, save for where the court imputes, or imposes upon them, what they would have agreed, in the absence of evidence. This is used for the quantification of the share. You need to look for:

- Common intention/bargain.
- Detrimental reliance.
- Unconscionable denial of interest/right.

Constructive trusts can be implied or express. There are 4 seminal cases.

- *Stack v Dowden [2007] 1 FLR 1858*: jointly owned property: quantifying shares

- *Jones v Kernott [2012] 1 FLR 45*: a fresh agreement and ambulatory trusts, or a trust that changes over time by means of fresh agreement;

- *Oxley v Hiscock [2004] 2 FLR 669*: for sole name properties, where the claimant is trying to prove they have an interest;

- *Marr v Collie [2017] UKPC 17:* in this case there was a conflict between one party claiming a constructive trust by agreement and the conveyance being in joint names, and the other claiming a resulting trust derived from contributions; the Privy Council found that intention was everything, however it was analysed and no one system of analysis " trumped" the other; *constructive trusts are not limited to domestic cohabiting relationships.* The case was sent back for reconsideration of the parties intentions.

The most important paragraphs in the most seminal case are probably these:

Paragraphs 69- 70 from Stack v Dowden supra:

"69. In law, "context is everything" and the domestic context is very different from the commercial world. Each case will turn on its own facts. Many more factors than financial contributions may be relevant to divining the parties' true intentions. These include: any advice or discussions at the time of the transfer which cast light upon their intentions then; the reasons why the home was acquired in their joint names; the reasons why (if it be the case) the survivor was authorised to give a receipt for the capital moneys; the purpose for which the home was acquired; the nature of the parties' relationship; whether they had children for whom they both had responsibility to provide a home; how the purchase was financed, both initially and subsequently; how the parties arranged their finances, whether separately or together or a bit of both; how they discharged the outgoings on the property and their other household expenses. When a couple are joint owners of the home and jointly liable for the mortgage, the inferences to be drawn from who pays for what may be very different from the inferences to be drawn when only one is owner of the home. The arithmetical calculation of how much was paid by each is also likely to be less important. It will be easier to draw the inference that they intended that each should contribute as much to the household as they reasonably could and that they would share the eventual benefit or burden equally. The parties' individual characters and personalities may also be a factor in deciding where their true intentions lay. In the cohabitation context, mercenary considerations may be more to the fore than they would be in marriage, but it should not be assumed that they always take pride of place over natural love and affection. At the end of the day, having taken all this into account, cases in which the joint legal

owners are to be taken to have intended that their beneficial interests should be different from their legal interests will be very unusual.

70. This is not, of course, an exhaustive list. There may also be reason to conclude that, whatever the parties' intentions at the outset, these have now changed. An example might be where one party has financed (or constructed himself) an extension or substantial improvement to the property, so that what they have now is significantly different from what they had then"

So, where it is established by law or beneficial interest that there is joint ownership and shares, but they are unquantified shares, the Court should look to what the parties decided and intended and look for evidence of that. If that is not there, then it should consider what they would have said if it had been expressed i.e. infer what was agreed.

If there is no evidence of it then the Court should impute what the Court believes is fair. At this point the Supreme Court Justices fall out a bit: and some in *Jones v Kernott [2012] 1 AC 776 (Lord Collins)* disagree; my advice is to stick with para 126 and Baroness Hale's judgment which is held to be the leading judgment and Lord Kerr agreed with her.

Helpful checklist

- Where the beneficial interests are not declared somewhere on paper such as the TR1 or a trust deed at purchase or after, the presumption is that equity follows the law and the beneficial interests reflect the legal interests in the property.

- The onus is upon the person who seeks to show it is different to prove that and it will be only be a very unusual case where they manage to do so;

- The onus of rebutting the presumption will be heavier in joint names cases than in sole name cases:

Lady Hale in *Stack*:

"69 At the end of the day … cases in which the joint legal owners are to be taken to have intended that their beneficial interests should be different from their legal interests will be very unusual."

- If the presumption that beneficial ownership reflects the legal ownership is rebutted, the court will search for what the parties intended as to the quantification of shares. They will look at the evidence in the light of the parties' conduct. It is not what the Court thinks is fair buy what did the parties intended at the time or thereafter.

Joint names cases

Where a property, intended to become their home, is conveyed *into the joint names* of a cohabiting couple, without an express declaration as to their beneficial interests, there will be a rebuttable presumption of a beneficial joint tenancy which when severed is held in equal shares as tenants in common.

- Baroness Hale in Stack 66: The questions in a joint names case are not simply "*what is the extent of the parties' beneficial interests?*" but (a) "*did the parties intend their beneficial interest to be different from their legal interests?*" and (b) "*if they did, in what way and to what extent*"?

- Each case will turn on its own facts as the evidence of their actions and intention will be different in each.

- In cases where the transfer/conveyance declares that the survivor could give a valid receipt for capital monies arising on a disposition of the land, AND it is established that the parties understood the right to survivorship would apply the inference is likely to be beneficial joint tenancy unless there is clear evidence to the contrary.

Sole name cases

The onus is upon the non-owner to establish his interest by clear evidence.

- If the claimant has established (s)he has some beneficial interest, the court will survey the whole course of dealing between the parties, taking account of all conduct to establish the parties intentions as to what shares were intended.

- As to variation of an original agreement:

  The Court will consider evidence of a fresh agreement but it must be clear this was what the parties intended and if the first declaration was in writing, there is a dispute as to whether a fresh agreement can be orally expressed. Check the judgment in *Hudson v Hathway [2022] EWCA Civ 1648,* however, if there are e-mails or similar supporting the fresh agreement, as these might amount to an transfer of an equitable interest in the property under s 53 (1)c) of the Law of Property Act 1925 or even a transfer of legal interest under s 2 Law of Property (Miscellaneous Provisions) Act 1989.

Proprietary estoppel

Estoppel is where equity imposes a solution after the event.

This can have tax consequences as it is not the court declaring what the position has always been, by means of declaring what trust has existed, but declaring what the ownership position should be now, according to the law of equity.

It is a promise, by words, action or silence, to transfer or that the person will have or has an interest property. The promise has acted upon that promise to their detriment where it would be unconscionable to deny the promise, so it has significant cross over with constructive trust.

It thereby allows the Court to declare new interests in property, to estop the promisor denying what they promised and what the other person relied upon.

The court will declare not only the transfer but of how much, so the the share created.

Elements of proprietary estoppel:

Taylor Fashions Ltd. v. Liverpool Victoria Trustees Ltd. [1982] QB 133 sets out the 3 requirements of proving an estoppel case. This was approved by the Court of Appeal in *Habib Bank v Habib Bank AG Zurich [1981] 1 WLR 1265* and was applied by the Privy Council in *Lim Teng Huan v Ang Swee Chuan [1992] 1 WLR 1306.* Under the modern approach there are three requirements to establish an equity for proprietary estoppel:

i. A representation or assurance;

ii. An act of detrimental reliance;

iii. An unconscionable denial of the claimant's right.

Matrimonial Proceedings and Property Act 1970 section 37

This claim is often forgotten and it is different from trusts or estoppel. Contributions by a spouse or fiancé (e) in money or money's worth to the improvement of property may generate an interest therein if it is a significant contribution.

- *Section 37.*

> *"It is hereby declared that where a husband or wife contributes in money or money's worth to the improvement of real or personal property in which or in the proceeds of sale of which either or both of them has or have a beneficial interest, the husband or wife so contributing shall, if the contribution is of a substantial nature and subject to any agreement between them to the contrary express or implied, be treated as having then acquired by virtue of his or her contribution a share or an enlarged share, as the case may be, in that beneficial interest of such an extent as may have been then agreed or, in default of such agreement, as may seem in all the circumstances just to any court before which the question of the existence or extent of the beneficial interest of the husband or wife arises (whether in proceedings between them or in any other proceedings)."*

If the parties are engaged rather than married this section is still effective.

The main case here is *Dibble v Pfluger [2010] EWCA Civ 1005* where payment for a new roof on a Polish property led to an interest in it (all of which had been forgotten/ignored when the case had been heard first time around, before the appeal).

Equitable Accounting:

An account does NOT change the size of the beneficial interest, it is an equitable adjustment after the event.

Sections 12–15 TLATA govern occupation rent which may be demanded by a party put out of or excluded from the property, to compensate them for the person living in their part of the property. This is called occupation rent. The jurisdiction to order the payment of occupation rent to an excluded beneficiary under a trust of land derives from sections 12 to 15 of the Trusts of Land and Appointment of Trustees Act 1996. It is an error to order an occupation rent without applying those statutory principles.Lady Hale ruled (at 94 in *Stack*) that those statutory powers replaced the old doctrine of equitable accounting in respect of occupation rent. She stated:

> *"93 Section 12(1) gives a beneficiary who is beneficially entitled to an interest in land the right to occupy the land if the purpose of the trust is to make the land available for his occupation. ... Section 13(1) gives the trustees the power to exclude or restrict that entitlement, but under section 13(2) this power must be exercised reasonably. The trustees also have power under section 13(3) to impose conditions upon the occupier. These include, under section 13(5), paying any outgoings or expenses ... and under section 13(6) paying compensation to a person whose right to occupy has been excluded or restricted. Under section 14(2)(a), both trustees and beneficiaries can apply to the court for an order relating to the exercise of these functions."*

A party might, however, apply for an equitable accounting payment if they have been paying all of the mortgage since separation.

Accounting can also apply to payment of endowment policies or savings vehicles as well as the occupation rent[57].

Clarke v Harlowe [2005] EWCA Civ 857 makes clear that as far as property law is concerned, as at separation of a cohabiting couple the presumption will be that parties thereafter pay the mortgage debt on a monthly basis in proportion to the share they own in the property, unless there is evidence of an agreement to the contrary. If they have not so paid, then this does not change the shares in which they hold the property, but it is exactly the sort of adjusting payment which can be ordered by way of equitable accounting.

---

57 *Murphy v Gooch 2007 EWCA Civ 603*

Forced sale of a share to another party

Again Ss12-15 of TLATA 1996 governs selling a party's share in a property. There is no direct authority to sell from one party to the other, but one party can have first "dibs".

Bagum v Hafiz [*2016*] *Ch 241* and *Collins v Collins (No 2)* [*2016*] *2 P & CR 6* are clear authority for the Court having the power to sell shares in a property in effect by this mechanism to one of the other beneficiaries and see paragraphs 12 -19 of the first instance appeal in *Chaston & Anor v Chaston [2018] EWHC 1672 (Ch).*

Concluding remarks

Trusts of land claims are often avoided by the family practitioner although the circumstances that give rise to them usually come into their department as they tend to arise upon the breakdown of a relationship and there may well be a child involved, hence the Schedule 1 inter-relationship. I have set out above all of the basics you need to determine whether there is a trusts of land claim to run alongside the Schedule 1 case. Schedule 1 may provide a home for your client and the child but a trusts of land claim could provide an interest in the property or an interest to live in a property which does not revert when the child leaves home. It is an interest for the adult client, not the child. You will only know that, if you know what questions to ask the client and what evidence to gather. The clams are often run in parallel and the ones I have seen almost always run in the family jurisdiction.

You now have the tools to understand and run a Schedule 1 claim, and to advise on various other aspects that often arise in conjunction. Hopefully a few questions have been answered or your understanding confirmed. Schedule 1 does not have to be expensive if a claim is focussed properly. You might have a FA converted into an FDR, after only Forms E1 and no questionnaires. The costs are going to be proportionate to many cases. Remember, Schedule 1 is not just for special occasions or glitzy big money cases. Take it out of your wardrobe, and use it with confidence. You might not need it every day but when you do, it should serve you well. After all, it is already 30 years old and it knows what it is doing now.

'The Electronic Communications Code: A Practical Guide – Second Edition' by Kerry Bretherton KC, James Castle, Mark Loveday
'A Practical Guide to the Independent School Standards – September 2023 Edition' by Sarah McKimm
'A Practical Guide to Estate Administration and Crypto Assets' by Richard Marshall
'A Practical Guide to Parental Alienation in Private and Public Law Children Cases' by Sam King QC & Frankie Shama
'Contested Heritage – Removing Art from Land and Historic Buildings' by Richard Harwood QC, Catherine Dobson, David Sawtell
'The Limits of Separate Legal Personality: When Those Running a Company Can Be Held Personally Liable for Losses Caused to Third Parties Outside of the Company' by Dr Mike Wilkinson
'A Practical Guide to Transgender Law' by Robin Moira White & Nicola Newbegin
'A Practical Guide to 'Stranded Spouses' in Family Law' by Mani Singh Basi
'A Practical Guide to Residential Freehold Conveyancing' by Lorraine Richardson
'A Practical Guide to Pensions on Divorce for Lawyers' by Bryan Scant
'A Practical Guide to Challenging Sham Marriage Allegations in Immigration Law' by Priya Solanki
'A Practical Guide to Digital Communications Evidence in Criminal Law' by Sam Willis
'A Practical Guide to Legal Rights in Scotland' by Sarah-Jane Macdonald
'A Practical Guide to New Build Conveyancing' by Paul Sams & Rebecca East
'A Practical Guide to Inherited Wealth on Divorce' by Hayley Trim
'A Practical Guide to Practice Direction 12J and Domestic Abuse in Private Law Children Proceedings' by Rebecca Cross & Malvika Jaganmohan
'A Practical Guide to Confiscation and Restraint' by Narita Bahra QC, John Carl Townsend, David Winch
'A Practical Guide to the Law of Forests in Scotland' by Philip Buchan
'A Practical Guide to Health and Medical Cases in Immigration Law' by Rebecca Chapman & Miranda Butler
'A Practical Guide to Bad Character Evidence for Criminal Practitioners by Aparna Rao
'A Practical Guide to Extradition Law post-Brexit' by Myles Grandison et al
'A Practical Guide to Hoarding and Mental Health for Housing Lawyers' by Rachel Coyle

'Stephens on Contractual Indemnities' by Richard Stephens
'A Practical Guide to the EU Succession Regulation' by Richard Frimston
'A Practical Guide to Solicitor and Client Costs – Second Edition' by Robin Dunne
'Constructive Dismissal – Practice Pointers and Principles' by Benjimin Burgher
'A Practical Guide to Religion and Belief Discrimination Claims in the Workplace' by Kashif Ali
'A Practical Guide to the Law of Medical Treatment Decisions' by Ben Troke
'Fundamental Dishonesty and QOCS in Personal Injury Proceedings: Law and Practice' by Jake Rowley
'A Practical Guide to the Law in Relation to School Exclusions' by Charlotte Hadfield & Alice de Coverley
'A Practical Guide to Divorce for the Silver Separators' by Karin Walker
'The Right to be Forgotten – The Law and Practical Issues' by Melissa Stock
'A Practical Guide to Planning Law and Rights of Way in National Parks, the Broads and AONBs' by James Maurici QC, James Neill et al
'A Practical Guide to Election Law' by Tom Tabori
'A Practical Guide to the Law in Relation to Surrogacy' by Andrew Powell
'A Practical Guide to Claims Arising from Fatal Accidents – Second Edition' by James Patience
'A Practical Guide to Asbestos Claims' by Jonathan Owen & Gareth McAloon
'A Practical Guide to Stamp Duty Land Tax in England and Northern Ireland' by Suzanne O'Hara
'A Practical Guide to the Law of Farming Partnerships' by Philip Whitcomb
'A Practical Guide to the Law of Unlawful Eviction and Harassment – Second Edition' by Stephanie Lovegrove
'A Practical Guide to Costs in Personal Injury Claims – Second Edition' by Matthew Hoe
'A Practical Guide to the General Data Protection Regulation (GDPR) – Second Edition' by Keith Markham
'A Practical Guide to Working with Litigants in Person and McKenzie Friends in Family Cases' by Stuart Barlow
'Protecting Unregistered Brands: A Practical Guide to the Law of Passing Off' by Lorna Brazell
'A Practical Guide to Secondary Liability and Joint Enterprise Post-Jogee' by Joanne Cecil & James Mehigan

'A Practical Guide to the Pre-Action RTA Claims Protocol for Personal Injury Lawyers' by Antonia Ford
'A Practical Guide to Neighbour Disputes and the Law' by Alexander Walsh
'A Practical Guide to Coercive Control for Legal Practitioners and Victims' by Rachel Horman
'A Practical Guide to the Law of Driverless Cars – Second Edition'
by Alex Glassbrook, Emma Northey & Scarlett Milligan
'A Practical Guide to TOLATA Claims' by Greg Williams
'A Practical Guide to Elderly Law – Second Edition' by Justin Patten
'A Practical Guide to Responding to Housing Disrepair and Unfitness Claims' by Iain Wightwick
'A Practical Guide to the Law of Bullying and Harassment in the Workplace' by Philip Hyland
'How to Be a Freelance Solicitor: A Practical Guide to the SRA-Regulated Freelance Solicitor Model' by Paul Bennett
'A Practical Guide to Prison Injury Claims' by Malcolm Johnson
'A Practical Guide to Advising Clients at the Police Station' by Colin Stephen McKeown-Beaumont
'A Practical Guide to Antisocial Behaviour Injunctions – Second Edition' by Iain Wightwick
'Practical Mediation: A Guide for Mediators, Advocates, Advisers, Lawyers, and Students in Civil, Commercial, Business, Property, Workplace, and Employment Cases' by Jonathan Dingle with John Sephton
'The Mini-Pupillage Workbook' by David Boyle
'A Practical Guide to Crofting Law' by Brian Inkster
'A Practical Guide to the Law of Domain Names and Cybersquatting' by Andrew Clemson
'A Practical Guide to the Law of Gender Pay Gap Reporting' by Harini Iyengar
'NHS Whistleblowing and the Law' by Joseph England
'Employment Law and the Gig Economy' by Nigel Mackay & Annie Powell
'A Practical Guide to Noise Induced Hearing Loss (NIHL) Claims' by Andrew Mckie, Ian Skeate, Gareth McAloon
'An Introduction to Beauty Negligence Claims – A Practical Guide for the Personal Injury Practitioner' by Greg Almond
'Intercompany Agreements for Transfer Pricing Compliance' by Paul Sutton
'Zen and the Art of Mediation' by Martin Plowman
'A Practical Guide to Adoption for Family Lawyers' by Graham Pegg

www.ingramcontent.com/pod-product-compliance
Ingram Content Group UK Ltd.
Pitfield, Milton Keynes, MK11 3LW, UK
UKHW021238300926
15471UKWH00013B/640

9 781916 698772